THE CRAB COOKBOOK

THE CRAB

HOW TO CATCH AND COOK CRABS

by

CY *and* PAT LIBERMAN

MIDDLE
ATLANTIC
PRESS
Moorestown,
New Jersey

COOKBOOK

Manufactured in the United States of America

1 2 3 4 5 00 99 98

Library of Congress Cataloging-in-Publication Data
Liberman, Cy.
    The crab cookbook : how to catch and cook crabs / Cy and Pat Liberman.
        p. cm.
    Originally published in 1978 under title: The crab book.
    ISBN 0-912608-96-X
    1. Cookery (Crabs) 2. Crabbing. I. Liberman, Pat. II. Title.
TX754.C83L53 1998
641.6'95—dc21   98-3260
                                                      CIP

Special thanks to Rod of the Crab Connection, Palmyra, NJ, for his help.

Cover Design and Illustrations: Desireé Keane
Interior Design and Composition: Adrianne Onderdonk Dudden

For information write:
The Middle Atlantic Press
10 Twosome Drive
P.O. Box 600
Moorestown, NJ 08057

This book is lovingly dedicated

to our first great-grandchild

Casey Lauren Liberman

»« ACKNOWLEDGMENTS

The Crab Book, first published in 1978, has been updated and expanded in this edition to cover catching and cooking that most delicious of foods in all its American varieties. In writing the new edition, we solicited information from many people who deal with shellfish—people in fish and game and seafood marketing agencies and in the Sea Grant College programs. They generously provided information on regulations, crab biology and recipes. We received help from many; we particularly want to thank the following for responding cheerfully to our queries: Shirley Badial and Nick Furman of the Oregon Dungeness Crab Commission; James Falk and William Hall of the University of

Delaware; Paul E. LaRiviere, of the Washington Department of Fisheries; Kevin O'Sullivan of the Alaska Seafood Marketing Institute; Jerry E. Reeves of the Alaska Fisheries Science Center; John M. Duffy of the California Department of Fish and Game; Christopher M. Dewees of the University of California; Marie Holmes and Paul Zajicek of the Florida Department of Agriculture and Consumer Services; Jay S. Krouse of the Maine Department of Marine Resources; Juanita G. Gaskill of the North Carolina Department of Environment, Health and Natural Resources; Paul G. Scarlett of the New Jersey Department of Environmental Protection; Paul Sandifer of the South Carolina Department of Natural Resources; Vicki P. Clark of the Virginia Institute of Marine Science; and Amy Brussard and Annette Reddell Hegen of the Texas Sea Grant College Program.

One of Wilmington, Delaware's finest restaurants, Harry's Savoy Grill, owned by Xavier Teixido and managed by Anne Hood, provided two recipes created by Chefs Corey Waters and Joseph Misero III.

In addition, we received valuable assistance on various forms of household and office engineering, from the use of the microwave oven to the use of the personal computer, from Amy L. Healy, Diane C. Settle, Virginia F. Liberman and Lucille Milano. We are grateful to them all.

In any work with so much detail there are likely to be errors, just as there is likely to be a bit of shell in a pound of crab meat. Any and all such errors (which we hope you'll point out to us) are strictly our own.

Cy & Pat Liberman

»« CONTENTS

»« TO THE CRAB

Inside the amazing crab

Is an alchemist's kind of lab.

It will take what the sea has discarded—

Old fish, never highly regarded,

Sundry sea creatures, living and dead,

Like the tail of an eel, or its head,

And convert it (a fabulous feat)

Into crab—the world's greatest meat.

Ah, the succulent white meat he makes!

Those delicious, ambrosial flakes!

Well, that's why we urge admiration

For this most delightful crustacean.

1 »«
ABOUT CRABS

People speak of the seven wonders of the world. Without evaluating the seven, we claim the eighth is crabs. We admire all edible crabs. Surely, they are one of Mother Nature's most amazing creations. They take various cast-off vegetable and animal matter and convert it into the world's most delicious meat for humans. Without delving at all into the crab's secrets about how he (or she) makes this miraculous conversion, we are content to applaud the results. We praise the crab. We delight in consuming the meat of the cooked crab in many different ways. Some are even better than others. We have never made a crab dish we did not like. But, of course, others can manage it. And although

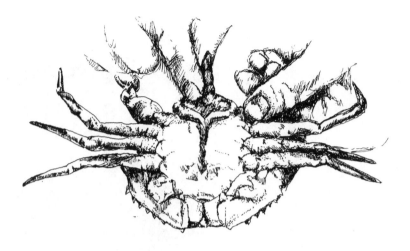

we were brought up on the Atlantic Blue crab, we enjoy the Dungeness, the Stone crab and all their cousins.

If we were put on diets that limited us to one kind of meat, there is no doubt whatsoever that we would choose crab. Actually, we've never had that limitation imposed, but we've often been near a good source of crabs we could catch ourselves, and we happily consumed different crab dishes for dinner every night and often had others for lunch. What we do in this volume is share with you our enthusiasm for getting, cooking and eating crabs of various kinds. We explain in detail how to do those three pleasurable things, where possible, with emphasis on the last. But we're not technical about it. We give the scientific names of the edible crabs just to be precise about them. If you want to know more than we report on the life cycles of the different crabs, or on their anatomy and sex habits (which do not set a good example for humans), you can readily find out more on those subjects in an encyclopedia. We're not greatly interested in the sex life of the crab. We're interested in having crabs know all about that and reproducing in suitable quantities so that all of us can be interested in the adult crab as delectable food for discriminating humans.

While the Blue crab of the East and South was our first love among all shellfish, we later learned that the crabs from other coasts are also delicious and can be prepared with the same or similar recipes. Some of the other crabs are less complicated to eat when it's up to you to get the meat out of the shell. We like Stone crab claws and the meat of Alaskan King crabs, Snow crabs, Dungeness crabs and also of those smaller crustaceans, steamed hard Blue crabs. We explain how to catch and eat the Dungeness and other crabs. We tell how to cook with crabs from all coasts of the U.S., including Alaska, which has more kinds of crabs than any other state. The emphasis, though, is on eating all varieties. That's the payoff. When it comes to recipes, all kinds of crab meat can be used—even surimi, the artificial crab meat cleverly made from pollock and other ingredients.

Now let's look into the wealth of delectable crabs in America and Canada.

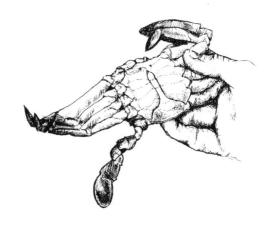

2 »«
NORTH AMERICAN
CRAB VARIETIES

The continental U.S., Alaska and Canada are well supplied with crabs. All the coasts have their favorite native crabs. In the East, the Blue crab is what people usually mean when they say, "Let's eat crab," except in Maine and Florida. In Maine, the most abundant variety is the Rock crab; both the Rock and Jonah are used in Maine's crab rolls. In Florida, the favorite is the Stone crab, although the Blue is also appreciated. Along the Gulf Coast, especially in Louisiana, the Blue crab reigns all the way to Texas. Louisiana ships its big Blue crabs to other states, particularly when the local crabs are out of season. On the West Coast, the local crab is the Dungeness; while in Alaska, the King and Tanner are the most heavily marketed, although the Snow crab and several other varieties are shipped to a crab-hungry world. Eastern Canada catches and ships quantities of the same cold-water crabs, along with Jonah.

Let's take a brief look at all these varieties, and their differences. First, about their general appearance. The King and Snow crabs have long legs, giving them a spidery look, while the Blue and Dungeness have shorter legs and are more compact. Crabs also vary in size, from the small Rock crab, whose shell (carapace) is often only four inches wide, to the huge Red King crab of Alaska, which weighs four to ten pounds.

In the long-legged crabs the main source of meat is in the legs; whereas in the others, except for the Stone crab, the best meat is in the body, although the leg and claw meat is also good. In the Stone crab, which has bigger claws than its cousins, the claws are the only parts used for food. The Blue crab in its soft shell stage is regarded as a delicacy, unlike the Dungeness and Red Rock; in their soft shell stage, their meat is considered watery.

A distinctive feature of Blue crabs is that they are swimmers—other crabs get around by walking. The Blue has flat pads on the back fins, used for fast swimming. There are other swimming crabs in the world, but none in North America. Swimming or walking, crabs tend to do it sideways, but not awkwardly. Another feature of the Blue crabs is that they like warm water and become inactive when their environment cools. All the many crabs of Alaska, Maine and Canada, of course, flourish in frigid water.

There are also differences in what crabs eat. Most crabs are scavengers, happily eating carrion. But not the Dungeness: it won't eat anything putrid. The Red Rock crab, unlike the Dungeness and Blue, likes to eat barnacles. We wonder if they could be put to work cleaning boat hulls.

Most crabs have ten legs—the biologists call them decapods. An exception is the King crab, one of those spidery crustaceans, which has only eight legs showing, including the usual two claws out front. So, crabs come in many varieties, but not nearly so many as those other tasty inhabitants of salt water, the finfish, and we crab fanciers have no reason to feel confused. Besides, in most areas there are only a few varieties to be found in the waters, and not too many in the markets.

Here are a few notes on the principal crab varieties of North America. The scientific name is given just to be precise. The popular names, such as "Rock crab," refer to different critters in different areas.

The **Blue Crab** (*Callinectes sapidus*) is well named since "callinectes" means beautiful swimmer and "sapidus" means savory. The crab is found in both salty and brackish water from Massachusetts to Florida and along the Gulf of Mexico's coast. Its top shell is a dull green and frequently covered with mud. The bottom shell is a dingy white. The legs of the male are blue. Males and females can easily be distinguished by the difference in appearance of the bottom of the shell. The female has an apron that is triangular while she is immature and then becomes dome-shaped with a point at the top. The male has a narrow band at the center, also pointed at the top. Both have sharp prongs, one at each edge of the top shell, which has eight short spines on each side.

Chesapeake Bay, North Carolina and Louisiana are the places most preferred by Blue crabs. The Blue is bigger than the Rock crab of Maine, but much smaller than the Dungeness. When a Blue crab is 6 inches wide it is viewed as a big specimen, although many males are larger.

The **Brown Box Crab** (*Lopholithodes foraminatus*) is a spidery crab found in deep water in the Pacific Ocean. This relative of the King crab received little attention until 1997, when there was a poor harvest in the Northwest. Before then, the Box crab was only harvested when the crab got into the traps set for its cousins. But when the others became scarce, fishermen went for the Box. A close relative is the King crab of the Northwest (*Lophholithodes mandtii*), not to be confused with the King crab of Alaska. Both are covered with spines, and both look box-like when their legs and claws are folded against the body.

The **Deep Sea Red Crab** (*Geryon quinquedens*) is found in the Atlantic Ocean, at depths of 100 to 1,000 fathoms, from Nova Scotia to Cuba. The top shell is dark red, and the crab is larger than the Blue, with a shell width of up to 7 inches and weight of about 2 1/2 pounds. The crab is often brought up by fishermen doing deep-water trawling for lobsters.

The **Dungeness Crab** (*Cancer magister*) looks like a very big cousin of the Blue crab. The Dungeness ranges in width from 7 to 9 inches and in weight from 1 1/2 to 5 pounds, with the most common weight being 2 1/2 pounds. The crab is found along the west coast of North America, all the way from the Aleutian Islands to central California. It is known under various local names, including Bay crab, Market crab, San Francisco crab and Dungie. The crab has a light brown or reddish-brown upper shell and a yellowish lower one, and has light tips on the claws. When cooked, however, the shell turns red-orange, just as the Blue crab's shell does. The crab is harvested by fishermen from May to September and, since it is cooked and frozen, it is available in markets all year.

The **Jonah Crab** (*Cancer borealis*) is found in Maine waters and in eastern Canada, and sometimes further south in the Atlantic Ocean to South Carolina. While it is the favorite crab in southern Nova Scotia and the Bay of Fundy, it is less abundant than the Rock crab, which it resembles. The Jonah is bigger than the Rock—in fact, big enough to make it worthwhile for seafood markets to sell frozen Jonah claws. The Jonah is less active and slower to move than the Rock crab, and it likes coastal areas with hard bottoms of clay, sand and rock, rather than the sand-mud preferred by the Rock crab. In some localities, the Jonah is confusingly called the Rock crab. It is also called the Atlantic Dungeness. Its meat is usually in small pieces rather than lumps. Some say it tastes like lobster.

The **Red King Crab** (*Paralithodes camtschatica*), one of the spidery crustaceans, is the largest commercially harvested crab. With its legs spread it may measure up to 6 feet, tip to tip. The crab weighs 4 to 10 pounds. Its two claws are different: one is a large "killer," while the other is a "feeder." In addition to the claws, there are six legs, containing lots of good white meat edged in red. The meat is slightly coarser than that of the Dungeness and Blue. The shell is light red, but turns bright red when cooked. The Red King is found primarily in Alaska, where it has two cousins, **Blue King Crab** (*Paralithodes platypus*) and **Golden** or **Brown King Crab** (*Lithodes acquispina*). All the meat goes into frozen Alaska King crab. Alaska fishermen, braving the North Pacific and Bering Sea in winter, bring the crabs in live to processing plants, where they are cleaned, cooked and frozen.

The **Rock Crab** (*Cancer irroratus*) is one of the smaller crabs. One advantage of that small size to the crab is that humans are not interested in the female, which rarely grows larger than 3 1/2 inches. Most of the crab meat found in stores in Maine is from the Rock male. The Rock looks somewhat like the Blue crab, but does not have the sharp spines on the edges of the top shell. There are nine smooth-edged teeth on the front edge of the shell. The crab is found from Labrador to South Carolina, but it prefers the colder waters of the Gulf of St. Lawrence and the New England states.

The **Red Rock Crab** (*Cancer productus*) is found in bays and estuaries of the Northwest, where it is favored by recreational crabbers and ignored by commercial crabbers because it is smaller than the Dungeness. It usually is only about 4 to 5 inches wide. The shell is red, and there is black on the tips of the pincers. This crab is also called Japanese Red Rock crab, or simply Rock crab.

The **Snow Crab** (*Chionoecetes opilio*), like the King Crab, has some very similar cousins: *C. bairdi, C. tanneri, and C. Japonicus*. All are usually called Snow crabs, or sometimes Tanner crabs. They're spidery, but smaller than the King, weighing 1 to 5 pounds. *Opilio* is the smallest of these; *bairdi* is the largest. The shell is oval and is an orange-tan color. The meat is more fibrous than that of the King crab. The Snow crab is fished mainly from the Bering Sea, but also appears in eastern Canada, where it is called the Spider crab and is the most important commercial crab.

The **Sheep Crab** (*Loxorhynchus grandis*) is found in the Pacific off southern California, and has been marketed only since 1984. It is one of the large spidery crabs with long claws. The claws are more prized than the body meat.

The **Stone Crab** (*Menippe mercenaria*) is the Florida specialty in the crab world. It is unusual in two respects. First, only the claws are used for meat. Second, when the claws are removed correctly and the crab is returned to the water, it can regenerate the claws, with the result that Florida has a self-perpetuating resource. The cooked claw is white, tipped with black and a touch of red. The Stone looks like a big cousin of the Blue crab, with oversized claws. It is no relation to the little-known Northern Stone crab (*Lithodes maia*), which is a spidery crab that has eight legs visible and prominent spines on its back and legs. The fifth pair of legs is small and folded under the shell. It is found in deep water in the Atlantic from Newfoundland to New Jersey.

3 »«
BUYING CRABS

There are two ways to get good crabs for your dining pleasure at home. One is to catch them. The other is to buy them. At the proper season, you can buy live or steamed hard shell crabs, and where Blue crabs thrive, live or frozen soft shell crabs. You can buy frozen King, Snow and Dungeness crab all year.

The picked meat is also available, fresh or canned. We have bought live or steamed hard shells from the watermen who make a business of catching them, but obviously we can't do that all the time, because it requires being at the right place at the right time. More often, we buy the picked meat—that's by far the easiest way. If you're starting out in pursuit of the pleasure of eating crabs, your first step—before you buy crabs to eat at home—should be to go to a restaurant that serves steamed crabs and order some, preferably with a friend who knows how to go about eating them. Yes, there are very detailed instructions later in this book on getting to the delicious meat of the Blue crab, and simpler directions for the Dungeness, which is larger and easier. As an alternative first step into the world of crab feasting, buy a can of fresh crab meat and make any of the cold or hot dishes we recommend in the section on cooking. That's an easy way.

When you're ready to buy live crabs (of any variety) for use at home, there are a few things to know. First, buy only those that are still definitely and visibly alive. Accept no dead ones, even if the vendor alleges that they were alive "a few minutes ago." You want them alive not only at the store, but until you put them in the pot to be steamed. Second, in some areas (especially with Blue crabs) the price depends on the size of the crabs. Usually, the bigger crab at the higher price is the better buy. Big ones are much easier to work with—you waste a lot in handling the smaller fellows. You don't have to worry abut the designation of sizes. If the biggest crabs available are called "number ones," they're the most desirable in most cases. What really counts in crabs is the amount of hidden white meat inside. There are rare times when a medium-sized crab happens to be more solidly filled with meat than a larger one which has just molted and not yet filled up his (or her) new and larger shell. When you have enough experience, you can feel the difference. It makes more sense to sell crabs by weight rather than by dozens, and that's done in many places.

Now, what about those roadside trucks with CRABS in big letters on the side? Okay for live crabs, if every crab is alive and moving. The same is true for little shops that specialize in crabs. We don't buy steamed crabs from any of those loosely rooted specialists. We buy them only from a source we can absolutely trust to have started the steaming process with every crab alive and complaining. If you have the time and a big pot, it's very satisfying to buy live crabs and steam them yourself. However, if you want the job done for you, try to find a place that will not insist on putting a lot of seasoning "salt" on the crabs when they're tossed into a basket or bag for you. Unless you've tried them that way, and know you like it, get the crabs without that hot seasoning spread on them. Instead, ask the supplier to put some of that hot stuff in a separate package. We regard that "salt" as a device restaurants traditionally use to make you thirsty so that you'll buy lots of beer with your crabs. Who needs it? Beer goes well with crabs with or without the hot seasoning on the shells. We wash it off if we forget to order them without it. Try crabs both ways and see what you like.

Next, about buying fresh crab meat. The first thing that may shock you is the price. But after you have picked a few dozen crabs yourself to get the meat for those wonderful crab entrées, you'll appreciate the labor it requires. Crab picking is what the economists call labor intensive. We don't mind paying the price for fresh crab meat when we want it and can't catch crabs.

Buy fresh crab meat only where it is in a refrigerator and is not only cold, but is actually sitting in and surrounded by crushed ice. That's the way it keeps best. Crab meat is difficult to keep for long; it's best to buy it where there's a steady turnover and careful management.

Fresh crab meat, picked by hand, comes in an unsealed can, often with a transparent plastic lid so that you can admire the white contents. The white may be speckled with yellow flecks of fat. You can also buy hand- or machine-picked crab meat that has been pasteurized and put in a sealed can, like deviled ham or tuna fish. If you choose the fresh crab meat—which we prefer—it must be cold when you get it. Then, when you get home, immediately put the can in a bowl, surround it with cracked or crushed ice, and put the can-and-bowl combination in your refrigerator until you're ready to make a crab dish. One alternative, of course, is to delay buying the meat until you're ready to use it. If the weather is warm and the trip home is a long one, put the crab meat in a plastic bag with ice, or take along a small icebox.

Much of the fresh crab meat has been picked by hand, but with mechanization spreading everywhere, even crab meat may be picked by machine, which sounds like quite a trick if you've spent much time doing it by hand with the smaller crab varieties. The machines use suction, centrifugal force and/or vibration. The resulting delicate meat is pasteurized, which is done by heating it to about 150° F. Then it's sealed in a can. Try it. And remember, you can mix it with surimi, the artificial crab, in both salads and cooked dishes.

We've talked about buying hard shell crabs and crab meat. In some areas, particularly where there are Blue crabs, you can also buy soft shell crabs in season. In other areas it is illegal to take crabs in the soft stage. Where they're available, soft shells are a special delicacy you can buy live or frozen—more often frozen.

The soft-shelled Blue crab (or any other) is in the process of molting and has just shed the old shell. In about three days the new shell will harden and the critter will become a larger hard shell crab. It is fascinating to watch as the crab extricates himself or herself from the old overcoat. The crab does it with difficulty and determination. The shell splits and the crab backs out, tediously pulling each leg and claw out of the old armor. Watermen and others in the crab business can tell when Blue crabs are getting ready to shed their old shells. Those crabs, called peelers, can be distinguished by a touch of color on the next-to-last segment of the back fin. The color is pink at first, turning red before the peeler wiggles out of the old shell. They call it the "red sign."

Fortunately for crab lovers, we can all buy good crab meat all year because of modern quick freezing. The Dungeness, King and Snow crabs of the Northwest, British Columbia and Alaska are distributed widely. A significant number of them come from Alaska, where Dutch Harbor at Unalaska, one of the Aleutian islands, is the largest commercial fishing port in the United States in terms of tonnage of the catch and its value. The crabs are delivered live to processing plants to be cleaned, cooked and frozen. When we buy the frozen crab it is easy to handle just because it has been cleaned and pre-cooked and is ready to be thawed.

The frozen King crab we get comes in packages of legs and claws and also in packages of "clusters" consisting of legs, claws and shoulder meat, adding up to about half a cooked crab. The frozen Snow crab similarly comes in clusters. The frozen Dungeness crab also comes as half a crab, with the legs and claw attached to a body section.

While we prefer fresh crab meat, the year-round availability of canned crab meat is definitely a big advantage, and the quality of the meat is high. Especially during the winter, we're all lucky to have the canned meat sitting on the shelf. It's pasteurized and will keep in the can for at least six months on the store shelf. When you bring the can home, you can keep it in your refrigerator, unopened, for another two months. Once you open the can, keep the meat well chilled and use it within three days, as you would fresh crab meat.

Nutritionally, fresh or pasteurized crab meat is about 18 percent protein and about 2.5 percent fat. A 3 1/2–ounce serving brings you 78 calories and about 80 milligrams of cholesterol.

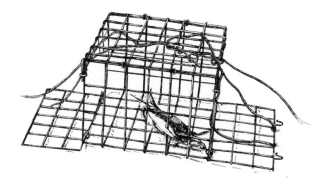

4 »«

HOW TO CATCH CRABS

One of the many pleasant aspects of crabbing is that people rarely lie about the size of the crabs they have caught, although they may exaggerate the number, or the time it took to catch them.

"Went down to Quaker Neck yesterday and caught two bushels of crabs in an hour and a half," a fellow said. He was referring to Blue crabs and to a quietly beautiful place on a tributary of Chesapeake Bay. We figured he was lying only about the time, not the volume. He used a trot line baited with salted eel, and he could have done about what he claimed, on a good day, not counting the time it took to launch his trailered boat. Crabs aren't like fish—someone once said the fastest-growing creature in all of nature is the fish, from the time an angler catches it until he tells about it. No, crabbing isn't like fishing. Ernie Ford said fishing is just a jerk at one end of the line waiting for a jerk at the other end. We don't feel that way about fishermen, despite the fact that many of them don't enjoy eating their catch. And that's a pity. Few amateur crabbers—except for children—are trying to round up a basket of crabs just for the sheer enjoyment of it, even if it is a pleasant occupation. They're looking forward single-mindedly to the feast.

The opportunities for recreational crabbing pretty much exclude the deep water crabs and are concentrated on the Blue, Stone and Dungeness varieties and a few of their cousins. The methods of catching those compact crabs are similar, but not exactly the same in all areas. The trot line is used by serious amateurs and professionals in Blue crab areas. Baited pots and traps of various kinds, and nets, are used in all crabbing areas. We'll describe how it's done.

Before you go crabbing, though, there are two things to keep in mind. The first is that you should handle live crabs with your unprotected fingers as little as possible. When transferring an individual crab from one place to another, use long-handled tongs and let the crab try to bite them, rather than your fingers. Crabs have speed and dexterity combined with remarkable sight in all directions. If you ever have to pick up a live crab by hand, grab its shell at the rear. In the case of the Blue crab, that's between the two back fins. That's the only place that is out of reach of the claws, which are amazingly maneuverable. In the case of Stone crabs, with their huge, powerful claws, don't go near them bare-handed.

The second point is that both recreational and commercial crabbing is controlled by state laws, which specify where, when and how you may legally catch crabs, and how many of what size you may keep. Get the current laws—usually very easy to read and understand—from the state agency in charge of game and fish, the same outfit that issues the fishing regulations. Crabbing is a seasonal sport in some areas, a year-round activity in others. For amateurs seeking the Blue crab, it is a warm-weather activity. That does not mean that crabs cannot be found in their habitat in winter. In Virginia, the professional watermen bring in crabs in winter by scraping them out of the mud where they are hibernating.

Crabs are found in salty water and in brackish water at various times in their life cycle. If you aren't sure where the little beasts are to be found, your best bet is to ask or watch the local people along the waterfront, or talk to people in bait and tackle shops or places that rent boats.

Bait

Crabs like to eat many things. Anything they like that can be attached firmly to a line, or to a crab pot or trap, can be used as bait. In Blue crab territory, the sport crabbers frequently use chicken necks, backs or wings, because they're widely available and cheap. Professional watermen are likely to call such crabbers "chicken neckers," but you have to expect some disparagement from the pros.

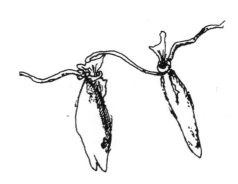

Fish heads also make good bait. Sometimes you can even get them free at fish markets if too many people aren't after them. If you're a fisherman, you may want to freeze your fish heads. Another excellent bait, with more lasting power, is salted eel, which is frequently used by professionals pursuing the Blue crab. Waterfront bait shops sometimes carry it, as do some commercial fishermen who put out eel traps. The eel comes whole; you cut it into pieces about three inches long. Keep it in a covered pot in salted water. Fish carcasses may be used for bait, especially in crab pots. But in the West, avoid cabezon—crabs recognize it as an enemy. The carcasses consist of the head, backbone and tail—what's left after fillets are cut from both sides. Rockfish carcasses, along with herring, salmon heads and clams, are used as bait by sportsmen seeking Dungeness crabs. The commercial crabbers operating in the Pacific use razor clams and squid for bait.

Methods

One way to catch crabs is to use a baited hand line and net. Obviously, first you find out where the crabs are and how you're going to approach them from above the water by operating from a pier, a bulkhead, a bridge or a boat. However, avoid small boats unless you know how to handle them, how to behave in them, and how strong the tidal current is. They aren't as simple as they may look to the uninitiated, but what you need to know to operate a small boat safely is easy to learn—on land, in a boating safety class.

Any kind of boat with an open cockpit can be used for crabbing. A small runabout or a rowboat is very satisfactory because you're close to the water and don't have to dip the net very far. But lots of crabbing is done from cruisers with higher freeboard.

What you need, besides the bait and some lengths of line,

are weights to pull the line to the bottom and a crab net. You can buy lead weights at a fishing tackle shop or use an old bolt or a rough stone that can be tied to the end of the line. Put the weight at the very bottom of the line, then tie on the bait a few inches from the end. No fancy knots are required. A simple over-hand knot or half hitch—the first step in tying a bow for shoelaces or a package—will be sufficient to hold a piece of salted eel or a chicken neck. An overhand knot will come apart easily later, when you have finished crabbing.

A net for crabbing is not something you can readily make. Simply buy one at a tackle shop or hardware or general store. Nets can be had with handles of aluminum or wood; either will do. Extra-long-handled nets are also available. The normal length is better for crabbing from a boat or most other places; use a long-handled net only in places where you have to stand or sit relatively high above the water. We use nets with cotton mesh. It rots in time but can be replaced. There are also nets with wire mesh. Either type will do with hand lines, but the wire mesh is preferred for trot lines, as you'll hear later.

To attract crabs, dangle the bait in the water with the weight touching the bottom. It's not necessary to hold the line by hand as you do with a hand fishing line. It can be made fast to any-

thing that's available—a post on a pier, or part of the gunwale
on a boat. Bait several lines and put them overboard at different
places. The procedure is to go to one of your baited lines and
pull it up very slowly. You may be able to feel a crab pulling at
the line, but sometimes you can't. In any case, it's wise to pull
the line slowly and cautiously until you can see the bait. Don't
pull it out of the water.

When the bait comes into view, if there's a crab working on
it, stop pulling up the line when the crab is about a foot below
the surface. It's time for the net. If you're working alone and
right-handed, take the bait line in your left hand and the net in
your right hand. Lower the net very slowly to the water, then
suddenly dip down and scoop up the crab and bait while pulling
the line up a little further.

You may miss some until you get the knack of it because crabs will let go and swim away fast when they see the net coming at them. But after a little practice, you'll know how to insert the net and how far to pull up the line.

When two people are working together, one can handle the baited line while the other does the netting. If you're using a light runabout or rowboat, don't stand up in the boat. Do your crabbing in a sitting position. The reason, of course, is that a light boat can be capsized easily by being unbalanced. Similarly, two people occupying a light boat can't crowd one side without risk of turning over.

You may prefer to put the net in the water before you test the line by pulling it up to see if you have a crab. Using that technique, you can try moving the crab and bait over the net before you swiftly swing the net up to scoop the catch.

An improvement in the simple cotton hand line can be made by attaching a piece of stainless steel wire at the end to hold bait that can be pierced rather than tied on, such as a fish head. Use a piece about 18 inches long and also find a piece of plastic tubing with an inside diameter just sufficient to hold two pieces of the stainless wire.

After attaching one end of the wire to the crab line, put the plastic tube on the wire near the same end. Pierce the bait with the wire and then put the free end through the tube to make a loop. Finally, attach a weight to the line. A good way to do that is to use a swivel out of a fisherman's box.

If there's no stainless steel wire handy, use a coat hanger. And if there's no plastic tubing, twist the ends of the wire together to form the loop after you have put the bait on.

When you put out several baited lines, the procedure is to test each one occasionally—not every minute. Take your time. Enjoy the air. See how the crabs are biting. Adjust the time you take to make the circuit among the lines according to the results you are getting. If you have seen no crabs after about 20 minutes, do something else for a while and try again later.

Opinion varies on when the best time to crab is, in relation to the tide. Some people say crabs are hungry all the time, like teenage boys. In crabbing from a pier, we think we get the best results when the current is running just before and after the high tide. But try crabbing anytime you wish. And don't worry about the phase of the moon. When crabs are in the area where you're trying to catch them, they seem to be ready for tasty morsels regardless of whether the moon is waxing or waning. They move with the tide. The current may bring more of them into the range of your bait than still water.

Crab Traps

Catching crabs on a hand line is very satisfactory, but it does take a modest amount of skill in using the net. Using a collapsible crab trap, on the other hand, requires virtually no skill and is less of a sport. But it often catches dinner. The typical crab trap

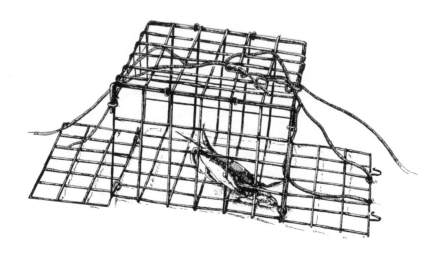

is a box made of wire mesh. Its sides—usually four—are hinged to the bottom. The contraption is rigged up with strings attached to the tops of each of the sides. These are attached to a single cord that the crabber holds. When the trap is lowered to the bottom, the sides flap open, baring the trap's mesh base with bait attached. A jerk on the string by the crabber quickly pulls the sides to their closed position and traps any crab who has ventured onto the base to check out the bait. The crabber periodically hauls up his trap to see if a crab has been caught—or perhaps two at once. It's a beautiful system, when the crabs are there.

The procedure is delightfully simple. Tie the bait securely to the base or bottom of the wire box using cord or wire. Chicken necks, backs or wings, fish heads or whole fish can be used. Then hold the line while you drop the box into the water and lower it to the bottom, as with the hand line. Be sure to let out some more line so that the sides open. Then relax. Give the crabs time to find the bait. After a few minutes, jerk the line firmly to close the trap, pull it up and see what you have. If you have a crab, empty the trap by letting one side open and shaking out the crab into a basket, bucket or other container.

When crabbing with either a hand line or a trap, you'll need such a container to carry your catch. In trying to empty the cotton mesh net, have a little patience. The crab will hang on until he sees where he's going, and it helps to let him touch the bottom of the container where you want him to rest. Don't use your fingers to get the crab to unlock his hold on the net—you'll be bitten. We take along a pair of metal tongs to use in picking up the crabs to measure them for legal size, sorting them out and returning to the sea those we can't keep. We tell them to grow up and come back later. The tongs are also excellent for convincing a reluctant crab to let go of the net or to get back in the basket. If you are crabbing from a pier or bulkhead, it's prudent to tie the basket or bucket to something firm to keep it from being kicked overboard in the excitement.

We find that box traps work pretty well. Some are three-sided rather than four-sided. They're satisfactory. It doesn't seem to matter to the crabs, so it doesn't matter to us.

Another ingenious variety of crab trap is called a ring net. This type, popular along the Pacific coast, consists of two metal hoops, connected by cotton or nylon mesh or netting to form a basket. The upper hoop is larger than the bottom one. The sides and bottom of the ring net are covered with the netting, and lines serving as a handle are attached to the top ring. When the device is lifted by the handle, it extends into its basket shape. When baited and lowered to the bottom it lies flat, giving walking crabs an easy path to the bait.

The ring net is used in the same manner as a metal trap, except that it should be hauled up rapidly to keep the crabs from escaping. These traps can be used from boats and also from docks and piers.

Crab Pots

Another device for catching crabs is called the crab pot. In some areas there are "folding pots" which, in other places, would be designated traps. Call them what you like. The non-folding types are called crab pots.

Commercial crabbers trap most of their crabs in crab pots, and that's without doubt the most efficient way to catch them— if you can do it legally where you intend to crab. There are restrictions on the use of pots in several states; in some, it is difficult or impossible for non-residents to use crab pots for recreational crabbing.

The crab pot is rigid and is larger and heavier than other crab

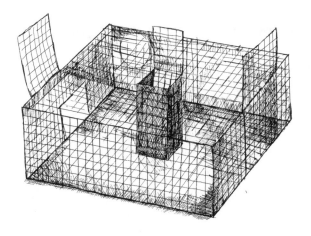

traps. Those used for Blue crabs look like boxes, about 24 to 30 inches on each side, made of zinc-coated wire that resembles chicken wire in shape. The sides are not hinged—only part of the top is. The pot has openings big enough for a crab to enter. Each opening is at the wide end of a mesh funnel the crab can go through. There may be two, three or four such funnel-shaped entrances. The inside ends of the funnels are flattened ellipses. Crabs swim into these entrances because they are heading for bait placed inside the pot in a cylindrical container of finer mesh. The pot also has a mesh partition separating the top section from the bottom, and this partition has two funnels opening from the bottom.

After a crab swims into the bottom of the pot and helps himself to some of the bait, he finds it mighty difficult to get in just the right position to go out through the narrow end of the funnel, even though he came in that way. In looking for a way out, the crab is very likely to go into the wide openings of the funnel entrances to the upper part and to end up there. Few crabs find their way out of the maze the pot presents to them. There's not much of a trick to shaking the crabs out of the pot. One section of the top opens for that purpose.

The beauty of the crab pot is that it operates unattended. Once you put the baited pot in the water, you can leave it and come back later, at your convenience. Commercial crabbers set out large numbers of them attached to marked buoys and make the rounds of emptying and rebaiting the pots.

We kept a pot working at the end of our pier and usually checked it each morning and late afternoon for a close-to-effortless harvesting of the best food the sea offers. With commercial crabbers, however, there's a great deal of hard work in pulling up the pots, shaking the crabs out, sorting them, putting in new bait as needed, and hauling the crabs to market. We salute them.

The crab pots used on the Pacific coast differ from Eastern pots in that escape rings are required. Also, many Western pots are much heavier and larger than the kind used in the East. While light pots can be used in many parts of Puget Sound, pots weighing 75 to 150 pounds are needed in the ocean and coastal bays, where wave action and strong currents threaten to move them. These pots are too heavy for sport crabbing. Commercial crabbers lift them with hydraulic cranes. Their pots can be huge—some are seven feet square at the bottom and weigh 800 pounds empty.

The Trot Line

Many watermen use trot lines to catch Blue crabs in volume, and so do some amateurs who crab frequently and have the space to keep the messy equipment. A trot line can be pictured as a very long line with many baits. The baits—usually salted eel—may be tied directly to the main line or to a series of auxiliary lines spaced along its length.

A trot line can be any length that is convenient. Usually it's at least 100 feet long. It can be made of any material, but it has to be strong enough to withstand a fair amount of tugging. Cotton cord one-eighth of an inch thick will do.

To set up a trot line you will need, in addition to the length of cord, enough baits to attach every three feet or so, plus two buoys and two anchors. The buoys can be plastic bottles. The rig is made up by tying one anchor to one end of the line and then fastening a buoy, leaving enough room between the two so that at high tide the buoy will float where you want to put out the line. Measure out the desired length of line and put a similar arrangement on the other end—a buoy followed by an anchor. The entire rig, with baits attached, can be coiled and put in a barrel or tub covered with heavily salted water. The trot line is best used with a motorboat with low freeboard, although it can be used with a rowboat, a canoe or, in shallow water, without a boat.

Let's say we're going to do some crabbing with a trot line and a rowboat with an outboard motor and that we have a two-person crew. First, we select the place we're going to try our luck and skill. We prefer an area where we can put out the line across the current rather than with it, and where the water is about six feet deep.

First we throw out the anchor and one buoy, then we slowly play out the baited line as the boat moves along, making sure the line does not get caught in the propeller. When we come to the other buoy location, we stop the boat to drop that buoy and the second anchor. The anchor, of course, need not be a boat anchor. A piece of iron or anything heavy enough to stay in place will do.

Now we pause for a few minutes, as with hand lines, to give the crabs a chance to gather at the baits. Then we're ready to make our first run from one end of the line to the other, between the buoys. While one person steers the boat slowly, the other crabber picks up the baited line and lets it pass across one hand while holding the crab net in the other. The procedure is like using a hand line, except that the line comes to you without your pulling it up. You have to act swiftly to scoop up any crabs that are holding onto the baits. They must be scooped before the baits come up out of the water or they'll disappear. It takes some practice for both partners to do their jobs. And it requires speed and dexterity to scoop up the crab, let it drop into your basket and have the net ready for the next crab. The best net for this purpose is one with steel mesh rather than soft twine.

An improvement in the equipment for running a trot line is to rig up a roller outside the gunwale of the boat, so that the baited line will roll up out of the water as the boat goes forward from one buoy to the other. Then the crew member with the net can turn his full attention to scooping crabs and will not have to handle the line.

If the anchors are heavy enough, a lone crabber working a trot line can pull himself along the line in a light boat. There are other variations on the use of a trot line: one end can be attached to a pier rather than an anchor, or both ends can be attached to posts.

When crabbing is finished for the day, the trot line is coiled and put in the barrel, tube or plastic bucket. The eel baits are sprinkled with salt and the whole rig is covered with an old piece of canvas or other material.

Baitless Crabbing

It is possible to catch Blue and Dungeness crabs, and their compact cousins, with no bait and just a net and something to put the captives in, plus a little skill. The "something" could be a basket floating in an inflated tire tube with a line to your waist, or it could be a gunny sack. You walk slowly in shallow water, usually at low tide, spot a crab and dip it up with a short-handled net. This obviously works best where crabs are plentiful.

In Blue crab territory you may scoop up hard shell crabs or soft shells waiting in the grass for their new shells to harden. You may even find doublers—crabs in the process of mating. In any case, you have to scoop fast—crabs are swift at retreating from your reach. But it can be done, and you can watch people doing it to observe the technique. If you try it, wear sneakers because, unfortunately, the sandy or muddy bottom is not guaranteed to be free of glass.

There's a handicap to using this method to catch Blue crabs. The places where crabs are likely to be abundant—in salty water—are the same ones that host the sea nettle, a kind of jellyfish that will sting you on contact. Wear long pants.

It is also possible to net crabs from a boat, particularly a shallow draft boat that can venture into marshy areas, sand flats and eelgrass beds at low tide. You may find crabs that have gone there to shed. In some areas, netting crabs from a moving boat is called "skimming." There are also places where you can catch crabs from a pier with a long-handled net and no bait. This requires water clear enough to see the crabs resting on the bottom. We have seen it done in a "salt pond"—an inlet from the sea—in Rhode Island. In that state, however, crabbing is for residents only.

The strangest method of catching crabs we ever heard of is called "Jimmy crabbing," and is sometimes practiced around lower Chesapeake Bay. A "Jimmy" is a male Blue. You catch one and tie a string to one of his back fins. Then you put him in the water and let him go to work for you, as a trained hawk works for a falconer. The amorous crab searches for a female ready to mate. Finding one, he cradles her. Then the couple can be pulled into reach gently with the string and both can be dipped up in the net. The female is removed from the male's grasp, and the male is ready to go back and find another. The best time for this is when the girls are intensely interested in the boys. In the lower Chesapeake this usually occurs in May. The reason for going to this trouble, aside from the sport, is that the females caught will be ready to shed and become soft shells. This is clearly not a technique for beginners, and the season for it is short.

While crabbing is mainly a daytime activity, it is possible to catch the crustaceans at night. Some people go to a pier or out in their boats and use a flashlight. The light, played on the water, actually attracts the curious crabs. The idea is to get them to swim within reach and then scoop them up in the net. The trouble with this system is that the same light that attracts crabs also attracts insects in greater volume.

It is also possible to gather crabs in a long net or seine. A net about 4 feet wide and 24 feet long, with poles at each side, is used in water up to about five feet deep. This method, of course, involves walking in the water and subjecting yourself and your partner to any biting creatures that may lurk there.

State Laws on the Blue Crab

Regardless of how you catch crabs, remember that you may keep only those that are of legal size and must promptly return to the water those that are too small. Give them a chance to grow up. To do this properly, you need a ruler or a stick marked to legal

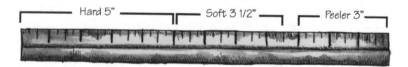

Hard 5"   Soft 3 1/2"   Peeler 3"

sizes. Some states issue a plastic ruler for this purpose. It's best to check with the game and fish agency in your state to get the latest information. There are, however, some sizes that have been in effect for years and can serve as a general guide—if your crab is smaller than these numbers, it's prudent to put him or her back.

For the Blue crab, the usual minimum size in states on the East Coast is 5 inches for the hard crab, measured from tip to tip of the shell. Many crabs seem to measure 4 3/4 inches, and that may strain your conscience. Smaller sizes are legal for Blues whose shells have not yet hardened: 3 1/2 inches for soft shells and 3 inches for the peeler (which is about to become a soft shell and grow). There are some differences among the states, and again, we strongly recommend getting the latest details from the state. However, here are notes on some of the limitations you are likely to encounter in the East when crabbing for Blues, along with the terms used.

Usually, no license is required of amateurs. Don't sell crabs—that would make you subject to complex commercial crabbing regulations. The state laws have provisions based on the stage the crab is in before and after shedding its shell in normal growth. Let's define those stages here even if you've heard some of it before. The *hard* crab, of course, is the crab with the fully hardened shell—the one we commonly see. The *peeler* is a hard crab with a fully developed soft shell beneath the outer hard shell. This is a crab that is getting ready to shed. The *soft shell* is one that has shed its shell recently. The *buckram* crab or *paper shell* is one whose new shell has become leathery, but is not yet quite hard. Avoid taking buckram crabs in Maryland. The *sponge* crab is a female carrying a mass of orange-lemon eggs on her abdomen, between the back fins. That mass of external roe is known as the *bunion*.

In **Massachusetts**, a lobster/crab permit is required for crabbing unless you are catching up to 50 crabs a day for use by your immediate family and you crab without pots or traps. Non-residents of the state who own real estate in a Massachusetts coastal town may obtain a non-commercial permit to crab from June through September, for consumption by the individual and his or her family. The season for crabbing is April 1 to November 30, and the minimum size for Blue crabs is 4 1/8 inches. There is no minimum size for other edible crabs. Crabbing is prohibited from 30 minutes after sunset to 30 minutes before sunrise.

In **Rhode Island**, non-residents may not take crabs. Residents may crab with net, trot line, or hand line in the daytime from May through November. The minimum size for hard shell crabs is 4 1/8 inches. Egg-bearing females may not be taken.

In **Connecticut**, the season usually runs from May to November 30, and recreational crabbing may be done by net, trot line or hand line or with personally tended crab traps. The minimum legal sizes are 5 inches for hard crabs and 3 1/2 inches for soft shells. Egg-bearing females must be returned to the water immediately. No license is required, and there is no daily limit. In Connecticut, there is more recreational than commercial crabbing, and no crabber may use the Chesapeake Bay-type crab pot.

In **New York**, there is no specific season and there are only two restrictions: don't take egg-bearing females and, in some areas, don't take crabs by dredging. Since dredging is a commercial method of crabbing, let's forget it.

In **New Jersey**, you don't need a license to crab with hand lines, scoop nets and manually operated collapsible traps. You do need a non-commercial crabbing license to use up to two crab pots or two trot lines. The limit is one bushel per day, and you may not sell any. Minimum sizes: 3 inches for the peeler, 3 1/2 inches for the soft crab, 4 1/2 inches for the hard crab the recreational crabber possesses and 4 3/4 inches for crabs offered for sale. Female crabs with eggs attached must be returned to the water.

There are also some rules on the use of trot lines and pots by recreational crabbers. The trot lines must be no longer than 150 feet, with no more than 25 baits. Both trot lines and pots must be marked to identify the owner. All pots must be tended at least once every 72 hours. No floating lines may be used on crab pots or their buoys. Fishermen with a bait net license ($10) may use a bait seine in crabbing but may not sell the crabs. No crabs may be harvested from the broad area defined as the Newark Bay Complex.

New Jersey's Division of Fish, Game & Wildlife offers a colored T-shirt featuring a blue crab and the legend: "I Love Crabs." It sells for $16 and benefits the division's ocean reef construction efforts. The shirts can be ordered from the Artificial Reef Association, Box 16, Oceanville, NJ 08231.

In **Delaware**, no season is specified for recreational crabbing, but it's a warm-weather sport because the Blue crab is not active in cold water. Up to two pots may be used from March 1 to November 30. Pots must be marked with all-white buoys with the owner's name and permanent address on the buoy or on a waterproof tag. Recreational crabbers may use a trot line (with no length limit specified) and may use any number of hand lines and traps. The daily limit is one bushel of crabs per person. No license is required. The minimum legal sizes are 5 inches for hard shells, 3 1/2 inches for soft shells and 3 inches for peelers. Females bearing eggs may not be taken.

In **Maryland**, the Blue crab flourishes in Chesapeake Bay and its tributaries, where there is even one area named Crab Alley. The crabbing season extends from April 1 to November 30. Recreational crabbers do not need a license, but there are time limits. You may crab from docks, piers, bridges and shorelines, using handlines and dipnets, 24 hours a day, but crabbing from a boat in Chesapeake Bay is restricted from 5:30 a.m.to 5:00 p.m., and from a boat in rivers, creeks and tributaries from 5:30 a.m. to sunset.

There are also limits on the gear that may be used. When crabbing from docks, piers, bridges and shorelines, you may use up to 10 collapsible traps or crab net rings or a combination of both. Recreational crabbers in a boat may use up to 25 pieces of the same gear, regardless of the number of people in the boat. An individual crabber may use up to 1,000 feet of baited trot line. Two or more people in a boat may use up to 2,000 feet of trot line. Crabbers may use any number of hand lines and may use seines up to 50 feet long if they are hauled up in the water and not on shore.

The catch limits are one bushel of crabs per person per day for personal consumption and not more than two bushels per boat. Mature female crabs of any size may be taken, but it is illegal to possess an egg-bearing crab. Minimum sizes are 5 inches for hard crabs, 3 1/2 inches for soft and 3 inches for peelers.

Note that the permissible gear for recreational crabbers does not include commercial crab pots, which are widely used by commercial fishermen and waterfront property owners. The latter may use up to two pots at their property. It is a criminal offense to empty crab pots belonging to another person.

In **Virginia**, there is no specified season. Recreational crabbers may use hand lines, the dip net and a single crab pot and may take up to one bushel per day. Trot lines and traps may not be used. The minimum size for the male hard crab is 5 inches, but there is no minimum size for mature females and soft crabs.

In **North Carolina**, the minimum size for hard Blue crabs is 5 inches from tip of spike to tip of spike. There is no size re-

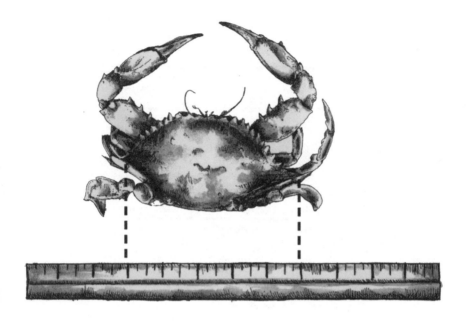

striction for mature females, soft and peeler crabs. The limit is 50 crabs. Recreational crabbers do not need a license unless they are crabbing from a boat and using one or more pots, in which case a commercial decal is required. A recreational crabber may use a crab pot from a pier without a license. Pots must be equipped with escape rings at least 2 5/16 inches in diameter.

In **South Carolina**, the recreational crabber may try for Blue or Stone crabs. Up to two pots or traps may be used in catching the Blue crab. The owner's name must be attached to the float, which must meet certain specifications on size and material. Female Blue crabs with egg mass must be returned to the water immediately. The minimum size is 5 inches.

With Stone crabs, only the larger of the two claws may be taken, and the crab must be returned to the water. However, no claw may be removed from a female with an egg mass. The claw that is removed must be at least 2 3/4 inches long.

In **Georgia**, recreational crabbers need no license and may use up to six traps measuring two feet by two feet or smaller. Each trap must be accompanied by a float carrying the owner's name and address and must have two escape rings, with an inside diameter of 2 3/8 inches, on an outside vertical wall. Traps should be weighted when used in strong tidal currents, and they may not be set in the channel of marked waterways.

The minimum size for Blue crabs is 5 inches for mature males and 3 inches for peelers. No minimum is specified for females. The bag limit is one bushel per day per person or two bushels per boat. Recreational crabbing is permitted all year.

In **Louisiana**, which is blessed with an abundance of large Blue crabs, no minimum size restriction is specified for recreational crabbers, although there is a 5-inch minimum for commercial crabbing. Recreational crabbers may use traps, trot lines, hand lines, dip nets or cast nets. Traps must not be worked from 30 minutes after sunset until 30 minutes before sunrise. Recreational crabbers must have a basic fishing license and if using crab traps, up to the limit of ten, must also have a $10 recreational gear license. If the trap is to be attached to a trot line, there is an additional fee of $1 per trap. Citizens of the state younger than 16 or over 60 are not required to have licenses, but they must carry proof of age. The basic license costs $5.50 for a resident and $31 for a non-resident.

Adult female crabs carrying eggs must be returned to the water immediately. Each crab trap must be marked with a half-inch stainless steel tag showing the recreational crab trap gear license number. Crab traps are prohibited in a few waterways.

Crabbing in Florida and Texas

Florida has a near-monopoly on the Stone crab, while also enjoying the Blue. So let's first consider catching the delectable

Stone crab, which offers meat somewhat resembling lobster in both appearance and flavor. Stone crabs are found in bays and estuaries, usually among rocks and broken shells, often in shallow water, along the Atlantic and Gulf coasts. The adult crab digs burrows 12 to 20 inches deep.

The season runs from October 16 to May 14. To use more than five traps you need a "saltwater product" license with "restricted species" and Stone crab endorsements. Some recreational crabbers catch the Stone crab by hand in shallow water, but this is a dangerous sport since the crab can cut off a human finger. Similarly dangerous is scuba diving for Stone crabs in deep water.

Unlike the Blue, Dungeness and similar crabs, the whole Stone crab is not taken. Only the claws are removed. The crabs are then returned to the water, where they regenerate the claws. Claws that are removed must be at least 2 3/4 inches long. You have to know how to snap off the claw without killing the crab. The daily recreational bag is one gallon of claws per person or two gallons per vessel, whichever is less.

Commercial fishermen sell the claws to dealers who boil them in fresh water. This is done because it is not feasible to ice or freeze the claws; that makes the meat stick to the shell. Once cooked, however, the claws can be iced or frozen and stored. You can buy them fresh or frozen, and we strongly recommend buying your crab claws or eating them in a restaurant rather than trying to catch the menacing crab. We do not offer directions for catching these crabs by hand or handling them live in any way. Eat them fairly early in the season; they become scarce in April.

You need a recreational license to go after either the Stone or Blue crab in Florida. In the case of the Blue, you must have endorsements similar to those for the Stone crab if you want to use more than five traps. The bag limit for Blues is ten gallons of crabs per day. The season is open all year and there is no size or sex restriction, but harvesting of egg-bearing crabs is prohibited. For Florida residents, a one-year saltwater fishing license goes for $12. Non-residents may buy a three-day license for $5, a seven-day license for $15, or a license for one year for $30. In each case, the tax collector or bait and tackle shop that sells you the license may charge a service fee of $1.50 or $2.

In **Texas**, recreational crabbers go for both the Stone and Blue crabs. In the case of the Stone crab, only the right claw may be taken, and the minimum length is 2 1/2 inches. The rest of the crab must be returned to the water from which it was taken. In the case of the Blue crab, the minimum width is 5 inches. There are no daily bag limits for either crab. It is illegal to possess, buy or sell a female crab that has her abdominal apron detached.

All public waters are open for crabbing unless a fish consumption ban has been imposed by the Texas Department of Health (call 1-800-685-0361 for current advisories). There are no seasons or restricted times for crabbing, except for the use of traps.

Recreational crabbers may use hand lines and up to six traps. However, traps may be removed from the water and crabs may be taken from traps only during the period from 30 minutes before sunrise to 30 minutes before sunset. Each trap must have a gear tag not more than 30 days old. Traps may not be larger than 18 cubic feet, and they must have escape vents. Also, each trap must be marked with a white floating buoy with a 2-inch-wide colored center stripe. The buoys must not be less than 6 inches high and 6 inches wide, and they may not be plastic bottles.

The standard fishing license for Texas residents costs $19. It is not required for persons under 17 and senior citizens born before September 1, 1930. Other seniors need a special resident license ($6). The non-resident license costs $30 and is not required for non-residents under 17 or senior citizens from Kansas, Louisiana or Oklahoma. A five-day license is available for $20.

THE STONE CRAB

The Stone crab—there's a clever beast—
Break off his claw to have a feast!
Then put him back—obey the law—
And he'll regenerate the claw.

State Laws on the Dungeness and Red Rock Crabs

Laws regulating sport fishing for the Dungeness and Red Rock crabs vary within specified areas of a state. In general, the minimum size is about 6 inches, measured horizontally across the back of the shell in what is called the caliper measure—not tip to tip, but just in front of the tips. It is illegal to possess the crabs in their soft shell stage. There are also limits on how much fishing gear a recreational crabber may use, and requirements on the equipment used. Furthermore, seasons are specified, and they are not always the same in all parts of a state. All of this sounds complicated, but it actually is not difficult to get the written directions from the state and follow them. It's important to get the current rules from your state agency controlling shellfishing.

An excellent example of these written rules is the *Fishing in Washington* pamphlet (120 pages) from the **Washington** Department of Fish and Wildlife. Only a few pages are required reading for the shellfish rules. You need a Shellfish/Seaweed license; residents pay $5 (seniors 70 and over, $3), and non-residents pay $20 for a full license or $5 for one that is good for three days. Add $1 in document fees for the dealer. Residents 14 and under do not need the license. Don't just put the license in your pocket—it should be displayed on the outside of your clothing, like a hunting license, which it is.

Read the section on tideland ownership. Most Puget Sound and Hood Canal beaches are privately owned, and you need permission from the owner or lessee to take shellfish from them. Use the public beaches, if you want to operate from a beach.

You may catch crabs year-round with ring nets or star traps, or by wading, scuba diving or using dip nets, but seasons are specified for catching Dungeness crabs with pots in various areas. In most places the season is December 1 to September 15, and the minimum size is 6 inches. However, in Puget Sound the season is July 16 to April 15, and the minimum size is 6 1/4 inches. Hood Canal has the July 16 to April 15 season also, but the minimum size there is 6 inches. In all areas, the daily limit is six males. You must also retain the back shell with the crab and release all soft shell crabs. You can identify the soft shell by applying finger pressure on the underside of the shell near the front.

Next, there are limits on the number of pots, star traps and ring nets you may use in various places. In Puget Sound, Hood Canal and coastal waters, it's no more than two of these items. Also, every pot, ring net or trap left unattended must have a buoy legibly marked with your name and address and the number of devices attached—one or two. Crab pots must be equipped with a biodegradable device, such as an escape panel closed with cotton cord. The idea is to allow the crab to get out eventually if the pot is lost. The crab pot buoy is half white and half red, distinguishing it from the shrimp pot buoy, which is yellow.

For Red Rock crabs, the pot seasons and gear restrictions are the same. The minimum size is 5 inches and the daily limit is six of either sex.

Another example of state regulations in the West is the set from **Oregon**. There, as in Washington, the season for recreational pursuit of Dungeness and Red Rock crabs is open all year. In Oregon, that applies to crabbing in bays. You may use ring nets or crab pots, and you can try your luck from a pier or dock—if you have permission—or from a boat. However, the number of ring nets and pots you may use is set by law, and you need to get the regulations for the area you intend to operate in. The ocean is closed to Dungeness crabbing from August 14 to November 30.

Much of Oregon crabbing is done in bays, in water ten to twenty feet deep. You need lines more than long enough to drop your gear to the bottom—about twice as long as the depth. It would require an extreme amount of patience to use a baited hand line at those depths; it's easier to use a ring net or pot.

Ring nets and pots must be marked with floats. When you go to check your ring net (which should be done every quarter to half hour) approach the float against the current, and try to pull the net off the bottom when the boat is directly over it. If you don't, you will be moving the line before you lift the top ring, and the motion will warn crabs to dash for the exit. With pots, you don't have to take that precaution.

For Dungeness crabs, the legal limit is 12 male crabs not less than 5 3/4 inches. The female is returned to the water. For the Red Rock, the limit is 24 crabs of any size or sex.

In **California**, commercial crabbing brings in millions of pounds of Dungeness crabs. Recreational crabbers can also get their share of the Dungeness, along with its smaller cousins, the three varieties of Rock crabs. The yellow Rock crab is found most frequently in the southern part of the state, while the brown Rock crab is most abundant in the central portion and the red Rock is plentiful in the north.

There are separate seasons for Dungeness crabs in northern and central California; the Mendocino-Sonoma county line is the dividing line. South of that line, the season opens the Saturday before the second Tuesday of November and extends through June 30. North of the line the season is later, because it has been found that the crabs molt later in the north. The season in the three northern coastal counties starts on the Saturday before December 1 and extends through July 30. Dungeness crabs may not be taken from San Francisco Bay or San Pablo Bay or their tributaries. The minimum size for commercial crabbers is 6 inches, but for recreational crabbers it is 5 3/4 inches. Recreational crabbers may keep up to 10 Dungeness crabs.

For crabs other than the Dungeness, the season is open all year and the limit is 35 crabs. The minimum size is 4 inches, except in a few districts where there is no minimum.

People over 16 need a California fishing license to take crabs. The resident license costs $26.50. Non-residents are charged $71.95 for the year, $26.60 for ten days or $9.45 for one day. Reduced-fee and free licenses are available for eligible persons.

Crabs may be taken by hand, with the use of baited hoop nets or with crab traps meeting certain specifications. Skin and scuba divers may catch crabs by hand.

Crabbing in Alaska

Alaska has lots of crabs—Dungeness, Tanner and King—and lots of rules on where, when and how you may catch them. The state issues four different booklets summarizing the sport fishing regulations; rules on crabs are in all four, and they are complex. These booklets are issued annually—it's best to get the current one for the area where you will do your crabbing. One covers

Kodiak Island and Southwest Alaska. A second deals with the North Gulf Coast, Prince William Sound, and the Upper Copper and Upper Susitna River Drainages. There's another for the Cook inlet, and a fourth is for Southeast Alaska. All of the booklets contain maps and are well illustrated. They're effective from April 15 of one year through April 14 of the next.

In general, a sport fishing license is required to take shellfish for personal use in all areas of the state, unless you are a resident under 16 or over 60 years of age. The gear that generally may be used to take crabs consists of pots, ring nets, diving gear, dip nets and hooked or hookless hand lines. Crabs may also be taken by hand. Lines attached to rods or poles may be used only when fishing through the ice in the Bering Sea.

If you use a crab pot or ring net, you must attach it to a keg or buoy with your last name, first initial and address plainly inscribed, along with the name or Coast Guard number of the boat you use. No more than five pots per person may be used, except in fishing for King crabs (where it is legal to take King crabs), which has a limit of four pots per vessel. In some areas the season is closed to non-residents. Pots must include a specified escape mechanism.

Only male crabs may be retained for personal use. The legal minimum sizes and bag limits vary for residents and non-residents and in different areas. In the case of the King crab, there are different size limits and seasons for the red, blue and brown crabs.

Crabbing in Canada
Canada has the same cold-water crabs found in adjacent areas of the United States. The Dungeness and Red Rock crabs are in the waters of British Columbia in the west, while the Rock and Jonah crabs common in Maine are found in the eastern

provinces, along with the Snow crab, which is often called the Spider crab there. However, recreational crabbing is not permitted in eastern Canada.

You need a sport fishing license to pursue crabs in western Canada, and there are regulations similar to those in the United States. In British Columbia, a one-day license costs a resident $5.62 and a non-resident $7.49. A three-day license for a resident costs $11.77, and for a non-resident, $20.33; a five-day license costs a resident $17.12 and a non-resident $38.52. The licenses are readily available at sporting goods stores, resorts, marinas, department stores and from charter boat operators.

Canada uses the metric system in stating the size limits for crabs. Dungeness crabs must be at least 165 mm in width, while Red Rock crabs must be at least 115 mm. Crabbers are advised to use calipers in measuring their catch, measuring the widest part of the shell from outside the points. Females should be returned to the water as a voluntary conservation measure.

Crab traps may be used, provided they meet certain specifications. Each trap must have an escape section, a square or rectangular opening of a specified size, secured by untreated cotton twine no heavier than #120. A floating buoy must be attached to each trap, with the name of the owner clearly marked. Each recreational crabber may use two traps or dip nets.

British Columbia warns recreational crabbers of certain health hazards associated with the consumption of shellfish. Because of amnesic shellfish poison, caused by a natural marine toxin produced by a diatom, consumers are advised that the viscera of crabs should be removed before cooking. Dioxin and furan contamination has caused the closure of some areas. In the crab, the contamination is primarily concentrated in the digestive gland (hepatopancreas), which is usually not eaten. The advice: Be sure not to eat it. In some areas where the contamination has been found in crab body meat at excessive levels, harvesting is prohibited. Red tide (paralytic shellfish poison) affects bivalve molluscs, such as clams, but does not affect crabs.

The Live Box

Once you have caught crabs, you can keep them alive in a basket or ventilated box. Although they are creatures of the water, crabs can survive on land if they don't get too hot and dry, so put the basket in a shady, cool place. Put some seaweed or damp grass in the basket with the crabs.

Another way to keep Blue crabs and gradually convert some to soft shells is to use a live box. This is simply a wooden box with wire mesh sides and bottom and a mesh door at the top. You put the crabs in the box, lock the door and put the contraption in the water, tied to a pier or bulkhead. If you want to get soft shells, you have to look at the crabs periodically and remove those that have shed. If you don't get them soon after they're out of the old shells, the other crabs will.

Crab Hygiene—Safe Handling

Live crabs have delectable meat inside, but they are likely to be playing host to bacteria on the outside of their shells. This is not great cause for concern, but it is the basis for a few rules on hygiene when handling crabs.

The first is that cooked crabs and live crabs should be kept in separate containers, and the basket or bucket you use for the live crabs should be reserved for that purpose. Steamed crabs should be kept in clean containers which have not previously been used for live crabs.

Second, any surfaces that have had live crabs on them should be cleaned and sanitized. This can be done by wiping them with a solution of two tablespoons of laundry bleach in a gallon of water. Containers for live crabs can also be sanitized with this solution if you want to put them to some other use.

Third, if you touch live crabs with your bare hands, wash your hands well before handling steamed crabs. And by the way, if you want to pick up a live crab without getting a claw bite, pick it up between its back legs. Or better yet, pick it up with tongs or with a hand encased in heavy leather or rubber gloves.

It is equally important to be aware of toxins that may lurk inside the crab. There are safe handling practices that apply to all shellfish, as quoted from a publication of the Washington Department of Fish and Wildlife:

> Water color *does not* indicate shellfish safety. Cooking, rinsing, or freezing *does not* destroy toxins. Crab can also concentrate toxins in their internal organs. Clean crab before cooking. Eat only the meat. Eating shellfish with high concentrations of toxins may cause illness or death.
>
> Quickly cool your catch on ice or in a refrigerator from time of harvest until cooked.
>
> Cook shellfish adequately before eating. This does not destroy toxins, but can help prevent illness caused by naturally occurring bacteria or bacteria caused by pollution.

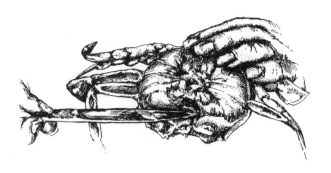

5 »«

HOW TO COOK, CLEAN AND PICK CRABS

After you've caught a batch of crabs and taken them home, the next project is to clean and cook them. Which comes first? With Blue crabs, we always wash the live crabs under running water, holding them one at a time with tongs, and then steam them before cleaning out (picking) the insides. With Dungeness and Red Rock crabs, the customs vary—some people clean out the live crab before cooking, others do so after cooking. In any case, the instructions for cooking and cleaning can be very brief or extremely detailed. We'll give brief directions for the Dungeness and Red Rock, detailed instructions for the Blue. All of the crabs are similarly constructed, however, so read both sets of directions and adapt them to your own preferences in preparing your crabs for the table.

Crabs can be cooked in water or steamed above the water. Dungeness crabs are usually cooked. Blue crabs are usually steamed. Let's look first at brief directions for *cooking* live crabs. Handling the crabs cautiously, put them in boiling, salted water. After the water boils again, cook for about 20 minutes. Remove the crabs from the pot and put them in cold water to cool before cleaning. That's it.

Cleaning crabs is easier and faster after cooking, and that system also permits use of a smaller pot. The following are the short directions for cleaning them: First, remove the back of the shell. Next, break the crab in two, separating the sections down the middle by folding them up and down. Third, shake out, or wash away, the insides (viscera) from each half under running water. Then scrape off the gills (sometimes called "devil's fingers") and snap off the tail flap. Rinse well. What's left is shell and meat, including the claws and legs.

Now let's turn to the detailed instructions for *steaming* live crabs. You will need: a large, deep pot with a steamer insert to keep the crabs off the bottom and out of the liquid; long-handled tongs for handling the live crabs; and smaller tongs or a grabber for removing the finished products. You will also need vinegar, spices and, if you like, some beer.

For one dozen crabs, put water—or half water and half beer—about one inch deep in the pot. Add two tablespoons of vinegar. That's enough liquid; crabs have a lot of moisture themselves. Bring to a boil under a tight lid.

Meanwhile, take the live crabs to the sink. Using the tongs, wash them well under cold running water. Transfer them, one by one, to the steaming pot, immersing them head first. They will be permanently subdued quite quickly. When the crabs are safely in the kettle, sprinkle them with two tablespoons of Old Bay Seasoning and a little salt, a bag of Zatarain's Crab Boil or your own mixture of spices. Use a tight lid and steam the crabs for 25 minutes.

There are other methods for getting the crabs from the basket to the kettle. They can be immersed in very hot water, which will quell their fighting spirit so that they can be washed easily. We don't use that system, nor do we numb the crabs in ice water to quiet them for washing. We prefer the cold running water, because we want to be certain that each crab is alive and kicking when we begin the steaming.

If you are planning to pick the meat for a casserole or other dish, after the steaming let the crabs cool to the point where you are able to work with them without scalding your fingers. If a good sailing breeze has just come up, causing a change in the crab-picking plan, do the preliminary work: remove the "devil's

fingers," the inedible innards and the upper shell. Then the crabs can be stored in a plastic bag in the refrigerator until the breeze has died and you're ready for serious crab-picking.

Seasoning

Old Bay Seasoning, a trademarked mixture which is called for in many recipes, is a very hot collection of spices. Used in moderation, this product is a time-saver for the hurried cook, but it is potent, so be cautious as to quantity.

The list of ingredients on Old Bay's label includes: celery salt, pepper, mustard, pimento, cloves, laurel leaves, mace, cardamom, ginger, cassia and paprika. No mention is made of the proportions, but if you get a very small pinch of it between your thumb and forefinger and taste it, you'll see how spicy it is.

We use Old Bay because it is so easy, but we have also often steamed crabs using a bay leaf, mustard, celery seed and a couple of cloves, with a bit of cayenne and salt. Try your own combination, but use restraint.

About Picking Crabs

There is one big drawback to the business of making delectable dishes from the crabs we catch: the crab meat has to be picked. Once you've spent hours at this finger-wearying chore, we bet you will never again question the price of ready-picked crab meat. You may wince at it, but knowing how long it takes to fill a bowl with those tender lumps, you'll understand.

Crab picking is an occasion when newspapers—lots of them—on the table are a must. The shells, cartilage and other discarded parts can easily be gathered up and neatly disposed of in the paper. The other thing you will need is a sharp paring knife. A cutting board and a nutcracker will be handy, but you don't absolutely need them.

When the crab-picking labor is finished for the day and you're not going to use the meat immediately, cover the bowls of meat with sheets of plastic or fitted covers and place them in a larger bowl or pan of ice, as instructed earlier for store-bought crab meat. We keep it in this manner for only two to three days. We're probably conservative; we're also always crab-hungry and we have never had any problem using however much we are able to get.

Eating Hard Shell Blue Crabs

TO THE COOK

The Crab's delicious by itself—
Leave hot pepper on the shelf!
Strong seasoning won't enhance the crab.
(It sells more beer and boosts the tab.)
If crab meat's what you want to savor
Don't overwhelm its special flavor.

About the classic newspaper-on-the-table style of eating hard Blue crabs, favored by many crab houses: it's messy. There is no way to keep hands clean and dry in the process of extracting that luscious meat from the shells and discarding the inedible parts. For real crab lovers, the messiness is part of the joy of eating, but for the uninitiated, it is likely to be an unappetizing horror. There is no elegant way to have a crab feast, but there are modifications that you can make without destroying the mystique. Your own house can be the best crab house.

First of all, newspapers have their own special sort of messiness—printer's ink—so we have revised the table covering. We use cheap plastic tablecloths. We serve those handy little wash and dry pads, along with a large supply of paper napkins. We heap the hot hard shells on a platter and provide a large bowl or bag for discards.

If we have guests who have not been introduced to hard shell crab eating, and who are apt to keep us from making our own feast by needing too many instructions, we open the shells just before serving and remove the "devil's fingers," the useless inside and the upper shell.

As we've mentioned previously, in the crab houses where

steamed crabs have star billing, they are served smothered with salt, red pepper and other lip-burners, so that a pitcher of beer will accompany every order. That high seasoning is often put on the crabs *after* they are cooked. It not only overwhelms the crab's delicate flavor, but it also reduces crab eating to an excuse for swilling beer at a proper profit to the management. Beer is a fine accompaniment to steamed crabs—as is wine—but let's remember to protect the main dish. Let's not drown it to extinguish fire-in-the-mouth induced by overseasoning.

Friends who have eaten crabs at our house marvel at the sweetness of the meat and exclaim at its subtle flavor. If you have inundated crabs with salt and cayenne in the past, try doing it our way—you'll enjoy more crab. Don't add any seasoning after your crabs are steamed. Serve them up. Give each guest a small bowl of lemon-butter, made with the juice of one lemon mixed in a half pound of butter or margarine.

For the hard shell aficionado, as long as there are more crabs there is no need for anything else. We like the assessment of a friend who said a great many crabs, followed by a general hand washing and a mixed green salad and fresh bread, adds up to a fine dinner for the fanciest of guests.

Our variation on the green salad is freshly picked corn and sliced fresh tomatoes. In preparing the corn, we line our large electric frying pan with inner husks from the corn, add very little water, bring it to a boil and steam the corn for about 8 minutes. If you can get both the corn and tomatoes directly from a nearby farm or from your own garden, you'll have them at peak flavor. Dessert with this meal has always seemed superfluous.

How to Pick Meat from the Blue Crab

PICKING

Oh, crab meat's a wonderful treat,
The most marvelous food you can eat,
But you know you must work to extract
That succulent meat that is packed
In the pockets locked under the shell.
In subsequent pages we'll tell
How to do it; but first comprehend,
It's worth every hour you spend.
So, patiently pick with your knife,
And prepare for the feast of your life.

And now we're ready for the nitty-gritty of separating the meat from the shell and other inedible stuff inside so that you can eat what you've caught or bought. There are many brief descriptions on how to do this, but in our opinion they aren't specific enough.

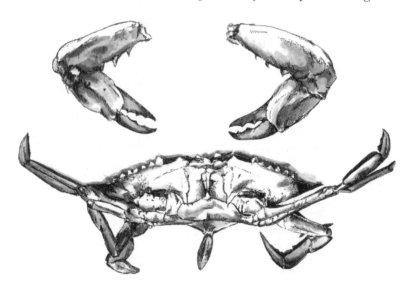

They're about as good as the cooking direction, "Cook until tender." So we're going to give a long exposition, one step at a time, in the hope that these directions can actually be followed by an uninitiated person faced with his or her first batch of steamed crabs. Get a paring knife.

Okay, the first step is to remove the claws. Not the four sets of legs, just the two big claws with the toothy pincers. If you're right-handed, which we'll assume, hold the steamed crab in your left hand with the claws forward and the one-piece shell at the top of the crab. Grab the claws, one at a time, with your right hand and pull them downward until they snap off. If any white meat sticks out of the broken claw joint, you're allowed to bite that off immediately as a small first reward for your labor. Set the claws aside.

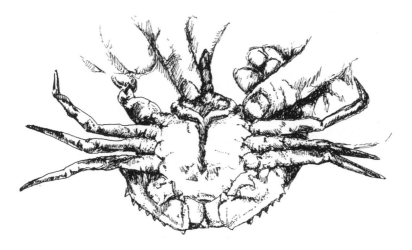

Next, we want the shell off. That's done in two parts. Turn the crab over so that the apron on the crab's bottom is uppermost. Insert a knife near the top of the apron—of either the male or the female, which have differently designed aprons—pry up the apron and pull it off.

With the claws removed, the largest fins remaining are the back fins, which have flat surfaces. Hold the back fins with your left hand, put a finger of your right hand under the shell and flip it off. It doesn't require a lot of pressure. Don't discard the shell just yet.

Put your knife into the corners of the shell, inside the joints, and see if there is some firm yellowish-brown meat there. If a lot of brown stuff hangs on, cut that off, and eat just the meat that

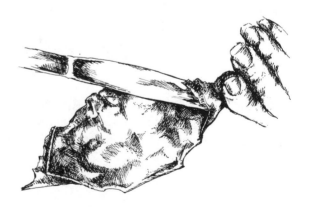

was inside the tip. It's marvelous. However, it's not for anyone on a low-fat, low-cholesterol diet. It's two very rich morsels—if it's there at all. Sometimes the crab has been caught at a time when those corners have not yet filled in. Crabs other than the Blue don't have those two sharp points where this delicacy is hiding.

Now put the shell on the discard pile—which can be a mixing bowl or a brown bag—and look at what's left of the crab. It will be a more or less round pad with four sets of legs attached. On two sides of what we'll call the top, you will see feathery, grayish gills, known as the "devil's fingers." Tear or scrape them off, using your fingers or the knife.

We're at the point where there's just a layer of shell separating us from the white meat. We'll soon get that meat, along with a little of the yellow cream, which happens to be liver. Some people call it crab butter. It's very tasty. Save some when you get to it.

Next, hold the pad in your left hand with the back fins at the rear and the top still up. Break off or cut off the front portion, forward of where the "devil's fingers" were. That front portion is the nearest thing to a head that a crab has.

Still holding the crab in your left hand, look at the top. You will see a central channel with assorted things filling it, none plain white. That's the crab's insides. Push that material, including any crinkly small items, out with a finger or the knife.

Now we have reached the stage where there are many techniques for proceeding to get out the luscious white meat from the pad. We will describe two quite different ones. In one, you leave the legs on for a while; in the other, you cut them off as the next step. Commercial crab pickers use the latter system.

In the first technique, which we'll call Cy's method of enjoying steamed crabs, you break the pad in half along the cen-

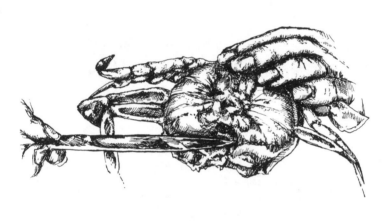

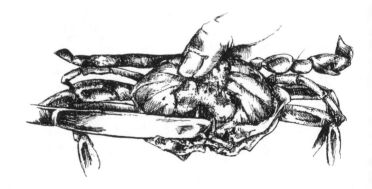

tral channel, leaving the legs on. Put down one half and take the other in your left hand. With the thumb and forefinger of your right hand, grab the half pad where the back fin is attached, putting the thumb on top. Press down with the thumb and up with the left hand to break off not only the back fin, but also the part of the pad that's attached to it. Try to support the top of the back fin as it breaks away from the pad, because inside the top is the very best meat of the Blue crab—the famous back fin meat. At first you will probably find it falls out of the shell. That's okay. Put it in the bowl where you're collecting crab meat, or eat it now. But after a little practice, you will learn how to break the shell while supporting the meat so that the back fin meat stays attached to the fin.

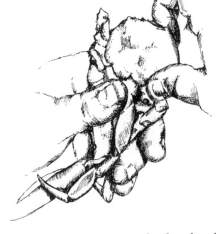

When you succeed in doing that, use your knife to break the shell away from the upper part of the back fin, the part nearest the pad. When that is done, you will have Cy's crab meat lollipop. Using the fin as a handle, dip the lollipop in your lemon-butter and bite off the meaty top. Mmm. That gives you the energy to go ahead with the work.

Next, proceed similarly with the other legs of the same half of the pad. Break each one off separately and try to pull the attached meat out of its shell compartment. Eat off the meat, or cut it off and put it in the bowl, or drop it in your lemon-butter container to eat later. Then break all the legs between the joints and squeeze them like tubes to see if there's enough meat inside to be worth the effort. Many people don't bother. We do.

Okay, now we're through with the legs—discard the pieces and go back to what's left of that half pad. Cut the half pad apart with your knife, cutting from side to side. The object is to lay bare the compartments containing the rest of the meat. Pick it out of each compartment with the knife. You can be as thorough as you like, or you can assume you got most of the white meat with the legs.

Then you're ready to go through the same procedure with the other half of the pad, starting with the back fin and proceeding to the legs. After that, get another crab.

From this introductory exercise, you will have discerned that the meat in the body of the crab, which we call the pad, is locked in compartments at the top of the legs and claws. The trick, of course, is to get it out of those compartments with a minimum of the walls, which are made of shell or cartilage.

Now we're ready for the second technique, which we'll call Pat's method. It's more scientific and rejects the idea of pulling out the meat with the legs. On the contrary, in this method you start by cutting the legs off and putting them aside. Cut them off close to the pad—even the back fin. That leaves you with a fairly neat pad. The next step is to cut sideways through the pad to open up all the chambers where the meat is.

There are various opinions on how best to make that important cut. We think the best way is not a straight cut all the way through the pad from side to side. Instead, try not to bisect the back fin meat. Try cutting down at an angle of about thirty degrees from the rear top of the pad, so that your knife will slit the top of the back fin area and come down at the center of the second opening from the back. That's the one next to the back fin opening. The object of this angled cut is to get the back fin meat out whole—in big lumps. Make that cut halfway through the pad, separating the back fin meat on one side. Then place your knife at the center line of the four remaining leg openings and cut through, parallel with the bottom, bisecting the pad's one side. Then do the same on the other side. Open up the pad, which has been cut into top and bottom portions. Use the point of the knife to nudge, slide or pop out morsels of crab meat.

That's the speedier, more efficient technique, to be preferred when you're picking crabs for consumption later, although you can use it for eating the steamed crabs immediately.

All right, if you're tired now, put the claws in the refrigerator in a plastic bag or covered bowl and get the meat out of them later. When you're ready, read on about extracting the claw meat and making crab fingers.

Picking Dungeness and Other Crab Meat

Now that we've explained in great detail how to go about extracting the meat from the Blue crab, you can apply much of the same technique to other crabs. With the Dungeness it's easier because the crab is bigger and the meat is easier to get to. With the smaller crabs, it's more difficult.

In all cases, what you have to do to get the body meat is clean the crab by opening the shell, getting rid of the gills and viscera and then cutting the remaining "pad" to expose the meat. It's in the channels of the shell, ready to be picked or pushed out of those compartments. It's work!

How to Make Blue Crab Fingers

Once the crab has been steamed, it is easy to break off the claws just by bending them too far. Similarly, the two halves of each claw can be broken by hand by bending them further than the hinge will go. Then you have four pieces of shell with good chunks of meat inside. That meat can best be extracted with a knife, and if you don't find that sufficient, get the help of a nutcracker.

Look at the lower part of the claw first, the part with the pincers. You will notice that one part is hinged like your jaw. You will also see, if you turn the claw over and over on any flat surface, that the claw has a curve to it. One side is concave and the other is convex. Turn the concave side up and look for a dimple or slight depression in the shell near the hinge. Press your knife point into that depressed area, about a quarter-inch back from the hinge. The shell is thin there and will crack. Once it has cracked, break off the non-movable part of the pincer, the part that's a portion of the main shell. Next, take hold of the movable pincer and pull out the meat that's attached to it. If you're lucky, it will come out whole and you will have a "crab finger"—

a deliciously good bite of crab meat with half the pincer to use as a handle. Dip that crab finger in lemon-butter or cocktail sauce, put the meat between your teeth and pull the meat from the cartilage that extends into it from the shell you're holding. A plate of those makes a wonderful cocktail treat. They can be bought in bags in some seafood stores; but now you know how to make them.

We get the meat out of the upper part of the claw by inserting the paring knife into the claw cavity and cutting the shell from the inside out. The easiest way is to use the knife as a lever, resting on one side of the tubular shell and cutting through the other. A nutcracker is also a satisfactory tool to use for the upper portion of the claw. Try to crack the shell and not squash it. A mallet is not a suitable tool; it tends to drive broken bits of shell into the meat, making more work.

Speaking of tools, the references to a paring knife were not more specific because any sturdy and well-scrubbed paring knife will do. It must be absolutely clean. In some states the crab picking houses are required to use stainless steel knives. The blade and the handle are made from one piece of steel, without a joint where bacteria could hide. That's excellent for commercial use, but it isn't really necessary for home use. We like paring knives with short blades and comfortable handles, and we wash them thoroughly in very hot water.

By the way, if you never experienced crab picking until now, you may have thought in the past that some sloven worked on that pound of crab meat that you bought and found to be not quite free of bits of shell and cartilage. After picking some yourself, you know better. It has always been surprising to us that, however meticulously we try to make sure not to confuse a bit of crab meat with a bit of cartilage, we always end up with some unwelcome invasion of shell or other unyielding material.

Anyhow, in the recipes given in the next section, the usual first line is omitted. We do not begin each recipe with, "Remove all shell and cartilage from crab meat." Rather, we'll assume you have been a fastidious picker, and that you will automatically check for any unwanted, inedible bits.

And here's a final question to consider after you have picked your first batch of crabs. Now that you've washed and soothed your tired, stiff fingers, how much would *you* charge for one pound of crab meat?

MY FOUR-LETTER WORD

If I have druthers on what to eat—
If I go to a very special treat—
If I'm asked what dish could make my day—
A four-letter word is all I say!
It's crab for me—C.R.A.B!

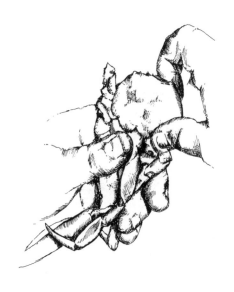

6 »«

COOKING WITH
CRABS

There are hundreds of recipes for preparing crab meat in many different dishes. Some of them are ridiculous, seeming to be the result of a crazy contest conducted to see who could come up with the most outrageous collection of strong spices to bury the delicate natural flavor of crab. Crabs with chili and corn flakes is one horror we read recently. We don't include that sort in the recipes that follow. In fact, we suggest the inventors of such disastrous dishes be awarded several nips from the pincers of the largest Jimmy crab around.

The recipes in this book give you a great deal of freedom to improvise, which is what you will find yourself wanting to do if you are crabbing and never know how large the catch will be.

On a really successful crabbing day, you'll want a variety of ways to serve your treasure. Revising the daily menu (putting that beef back in the freezer) becomes the order of the day when crabs are plentiful.

Incidentally, crab meat is a low-fat food. A three-ounce serving of Dungeness crab meat, for example, contains 1 gram of total fat, with no saturated fat. It also contains 65 milligrams of cholesterol, 320 milligrams of sodium and 19 grams of protein. It contains no carbohydrates, no fiber and no sugars. Crab is not a significant source of vitamin A or vitamin C. Considering this analysis in relation to a 2,000-calorie diet, crab contains 2 percent of the recommended daily allowance for total fat, 22 percent for cholesterol and 13 percent for salt. The three-ounce serving has 94 calories, including 10 calories from fat.

Ours is the ad-lib school of cooking. If we specify margarine, feel free to use butter, if you wish. In all cases where butter or margarine is specified in recipes we use a light margarine, unsalted spread or olive oil to cut down on saturated fat and trans-fatty acids, which the nutritionists tell us are undesirable for a healthy diet. When our recipe calls for milk, you may use half cream if you prefer a richer dish. In recipes where we feel cream is needed, we blink at calories. Be your own arbiter.

We have made some of our finest culinary creations with good substitutes. We keep a supply of dehydrated onion, celery flakes, dried parsley, herbs and spices. And we try to have a large assortment of standard cream soups for concocting sauces.

A standby that is handy to have for many crab dishes is chicken stock. It can be de-fatted, poured into ice cube trays, frozen and then transferred to plastic bags for storage in the freezer. Hereafter, when a cube or two of chicken stock is mentioned in a recipe, you'll know what is meant. If making stock does not appeal to you, use canned chicken broth.

But if you just happen to be stewing chicken to make a salad for that mob you expect on the weekend, do let the liquid cook some time longer, after you have removed the chicken from the pot. Then let the liquid cool, remove the fat, strain the stock and pour it into ice cube trays. (Of course, you will have remembered to add celery, carrot, onion, parsley stems and leaves, as well as a bay leaf, some cloves, peppercorns and salt, to the cooking water.)

Parsley is another of our favorite cooking ingredients—such a tasty green, useful in many recipes. When fresh parsley is available in stores we buy, wash and mince it and keep it in small, reclosable plastic sandwich bags in a handy spot in the freezer, where it will be ready whenever we want it.

Microwave Cooking

We use the microwave oven to prepare frozen entrées, thaw frozen foods and reheat leftover dishes. Unfortunately, we don't find the speedy microwave useful for cooking most crab dishes for several reasons. The directions for some say, "Stir constantly," and that's not feasible in the microwave. A few say, "Deep fry." Dangerous. In addition, we have been warned by a reliable chef that the microwave oven is very unforgiving when it comes to crab dishes. Unless you cook them just right by that fast method, the crab is going to come out rubbery.

Despite these reservations, we do include recipes that can be made with the microwave oven. But they do not include the one we saw somewhere for steamed live crabs. Can you picture trying to put scrappy live Blue crabs in a covered dish to get them into an oven?

We like to enjoy the advantages of both types of cooking. We think you maximize those advantages by preparing time-consuming dishes in advance and freezing them for later use, then defrosting and warming them up quickly in the microwave oven.

If you do want to try microwaving crab dishes, remember that all microwave ovens are not alike and that specified cooking times may not be accurate for your equipment. It's best to check the dish in the oven before the full time has elapsed to see how much more cooking is needed. Glass pie plates or straight-sided glass casseroles make good dishes for use in the microwave oven—you can see how the cooking is progressing. If you have no carousel in your oven, remember to rotate the dish.

What it all adds up to is this: You will find many recipes for the conventional oven (which we call "stove top"), some specifically for the microwave oven and some for both. Experienced owners of the microwave know best how to convert the one to the other, because they know the capabilities of their own microwave ovens.

However, there are two points we'd like to emphasize: First, with the microwave, it's better to undercook than overcook. Check frequently. Second, please remember that unless you caught the crabs yourself or bought them live, the meat has already been cooked. All you need to do is defrost it, if necessary, and then warm it for the table while cooking other ingredients.

Basic Sauces

Many crab meat entrées we like to make (and hundreds of variations you may create) require a basic sauce—béchamel, velouté or white sauce. Whatever you call it and however you modify or flavor it, if you do not already know how, learn to make it easily and surely.

The first thing to remember is to use a very heavy pot. In the dim days of mother's kitchen, a double boiler was used, but that is an unnecessary nuisance. We prefer enamel on iron or steel for a heavy pot, and have several casseroles which travel well from top of stove to oven to table. Heavy stainless steel or Pyrex will do, if that's what you have. Aluminum is not preferred, and do not use plain iron. The heavy pot is needed so that the roux—the flour and butter mixture—will not burn, and the sauce will not stick to the pan.

The next two requirements for a good, smooth sauce that does not taste floury (ugh!) are low heat and a few minutes of stirring with a wooden spoon or paddle until the butter and flour combination is frothy, but not brown.

The fourth and most telling point is heating the liquid for the sauce *before* adding it to the roux. If the liquid (milk; or milk, stock and/or wine) is hot and you stir it into the hot roux with a wire whisk, the sauce will never be lumpy.

Béchamel sauce is made with milk. Velouté is made with stock. That is the strict definitive difference. But in our ad-lib tradition, we ignore this boundary and often use chicken (or fish) stock with milk; and sometimes we use vermouth as part of the liquid.

For every two cups of liquid, use about three tablespoons of flour and two tablespoons of butter or margarine. Naturally, if you need a thicker sauce, use more flour. If you misjudge and make the sauce too thin, either cook the sauce longer, until you get the thickness you want, or add a little paste of butter and flour and beat it into the sauce on low heat. An even easier and just as satisfactory way to make the sauce thicker is to stir in some cornstarch mixed with water.

Now that you know the secrets of success in sauce-making, you need never be awed by recipes that require sauces, and you may even be ready to branch out and try your own seasoning additives to create new dishes.

CRAB GOES TO THE COCKTAIL PARTY

When the crab harvest is heavy, we enjoy the luxury of having our favorite seafood to spice up the cocktail snacks we serve to our guests. We often whip up a crab dip, rarely repeating ourselves. To the crab meat, we add mayonnaise, a choice of light seasoning, maybe a bit of finely minced celery. The result is the hit of the tray.

Another excellent cold treat for cocktail time is crab fingers, described earlier in the section on how to pick crab meat.

» CRAB MEAT WITH LEMON

If you have a good supply of back fin crab meat, or pieces of King crab legs, put a toothpick in each large lump and drop a little lemon juice on each. That's all. You get the unadorned beauty of the crab flavor.

» DEVILISH CRAB EGGS

Halve shelled eggs lengthwise. Set whites aside. Mash yolks thoroughly in bowl. Add all ingredients except salt and crab and mix well. Fold in crab meat and taste. Add salt if needed. Heap mixture into egg whites. Serve chilled.

6 eggs, hard-cooked
1/4 tsp. Dijon mustard
1/4 tsp. parsley (use dried, if
  necessary), finely minced
1/4 tsp. onion salt
1 tsp. curry powder
2 dashes Worcestershire sauce
Dash mace
Salt
1/2 cup crab meat (claw will do)

» HOT CRAB MEAT HORS D'OEUVRE

In a heavy pot, add lemon juice to crab meat and toss. In a separate bowl, mix all the other ingredients, add to the crab, and on a low heat, stir but do not boil. (A chafing dish is good for this.) Serve with assorted mild crackers.

1 cup crab meat
2 tbsp. lemon juice
1 cup sour cream
1/4 cup mayonnaise
1 tsp. onion, finely minced
1/4 tsp. chives, finely minced
3 drops Tabasco
1/2 tsp. Worcestershire sauce
1 tsp. garlic salt
Dash white pepper

» CRAB PUFFS

1/2 lb. crab meat
2 or 3 scallions, finely minced
1/2 cup cheddar cheese, grated
1 tsp. Worcestershire sauce
1/2 tsp. dry mustard
1 cup water
1/4 lb. butter or margarine
1/4 tsp. salt
1 cup flour
4 eggs

Here's a time when claw meat and shred and bits of other crab meat are as useful as back fin. Mix the first 5 ingredients together. Set aside. Combine the butter, salt and water in a heavy enamelled pot and bring to boiling. Remove and add all the flour, beating until mixture forms a ball. This is hard work. When mixture leaves side of pan, add the eggs one at a time, beating thoroughly after each addition. Blend in crab mixture and drop by teaspoonfuls onto an ungreased baking sheet. Bake 15 minutes at 400° F; reduce temperature to 350° F and bake 10 minutes more. Serve hot. This will make more than four dozen appetizers, fit for the most elegant party.

» TINY CRAB BALLS

Here's one of the few times we recommend deep fat frying. In this instance, it can produce a very interesting addition to your hors d'oeuvres collection.

In a heavy pot, sauté the onion in butter only until translucent. Add flour and stir in with wire whisk until foamy. Heat the milk and vermouth and add, stirring constantly with wire whisk. Cook several minutes. Beat the egg yolk with the seasonings; add a little of the hot sauce to the egg, then add this to the sauce in the pot, stirring constantly. It will be very thick. Add the crab and parsley. Stir to blend, then cool. Taste, adding more salt if needed. Shape into very small balls and roll them in the crumbs. Using a basket, fry in corn oil until brown (2 to 3 minutes). Drain well on paper towels. Spear on toothpicks. Makes about 40 crab balls.

1 1/2 tsp. onion, grated
2 tbsp. melted butter or
   margarine
2 tbsp. flour
1/2 cup milk
1 scant tbsp. vermouth
Yolk of 1 small egg
1/4 tsp. Worcestershire sauce
Dash cayenne
Salt and pepper
1 cup crab meat (body and claw)
1 tbsp. parsley, very finely
   minced
1/2 cup fine dry bread crumbs,
   or to taste

» CRAB MEAT IN MUSHROOMS

1/2 lb. crab meat

20 large mushrooms

1/2 cup melted margarine

2 eggs, lightly beaten

4 tbsp. soft bread crumbs

2 tbsp. mayonnaise

2 tbsp. chopped onion

1 tsp. lemon juice

1/8 tsp. white pepper

Stove Top Directions:

Rinse mushrooms and remove stems. Brush mushroom caps with half the margarine and arrange them in a greased baking dish. In a small bowl combine remaining ingredients except half the margarine and half the bread crumbs. Fill each cap with the mixture. Combine remaining margarine and crumbs and sprinkle over stuffed mushrooms. Bake at 350° F for 15 minutes. Makes 20 hors d'oeuvres.

Microwave Directions:

Prepare all ingredients as above. Cook on Medium 5 minutes. Makes 20 hors d'oeuvres.

(Based on a recipe from Texas A&M University.)

» CHESAPEAKE CANAPÉS

Combine the crab meat with the mayonnaise, bread crumbs and seasonings. (You may not need all of the lemon juice.) Toast the bread, then cut each slice into 6 squares. Spread them with the crab mixture. Place under the broiler for a few minutes, until brown and bubbly. Saltines or melba toast can also be used.

1 cup crab meat
1 tsp. Dijon mustard
1 tsp. parsley, very finely minced
2 tbsp. mayonnaise
Salt and pepper to taste
Dash cayenne
2 tsp. lemon juice
2 tbsp. grated Parmesan cheese
1 tbsp. fine bread crumbs
6 slices white bread, crusts
    removed

» CRAB SPREAD OR DIP

Here's an easy crab spread or dip that's very simple to concoct and is guaranteed to produce appreciative purrs among the hors d'oeuvres nibblers. After tasting it, you may decide on added taste embellishments. Go ahead, be adventurous!

1 package (8 oz.) cream cheese
1 cup crab meat (body and claw)
1 tbsp. butter or other spread
1/4 to 1/2 tsp. curry powder
Salt and pepper to taste
1 tbsp. lemon juice

Stove Top Directions:
Mash the cream cheese and mix in the butter. Add the crab meat and lemon juice and blend well. Add the curry and mix further. Add more curry and salt and pepper, if you like. Bake at 400° F for 15 minutes. Serve with crackers or flat bread.

Microwave Directions:
Put butter and curry powder in a bowl. Cook on High for 1 minute, interrupting once to stir. Remove from oven, mash cream cheese and mix in with curried butter. Cook on High 1 minute. Stir in crab meat and lemon juice. Add a little milk if you want the mixture to be thinner. Add salt and pepper. Cook on High 1 minute. Serve as above.

» TRY YOUR OWN

Unless you use too much of a spice, or a spice that is too heavy for crab, you will find it easy to try your own variations for crab canapés. Try finely chopped apple and celery, for instance. Tarragon, either fresh or freshly dried, mixed with mayonnaise and lemon makes an interesting diversion. Some people enjoy finely chopped olives and pimento as part of the mix. Who knows? You may happen on a masterpiece.

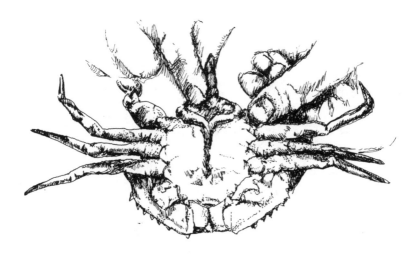

CRAB SALADS

Salads offer opportunities for innovative uses of crab meat to produce delectable dishes—and usually with no cooking. The most famous of these is Crab Louis (or Crab Louie), favored in the West. Let's start with a classic Crab Louis based on a recipe from the Oregon Dungeness Crab Commission.

» CRAB LOUIS

1 lb. crab meat
1/2 lb. Dungeness crab legs
1 1/2 quarts salad greens,
    shredded
1 cup light mayonnaise
1/4 cup chili sauce
1 tbsp. green pepper, finely
    chopped
2 tbsp. onion, finely chopped
2 tbsp. parsley, finely chopped
1/4 tsp. cayenne pepper
2 eggs, hard-cooked, quartered
2 tomatoes, quartered
12 ripe olives
4 parsley sprigs
4 lemon wedges

Line 4 salad plates or bowls with salad greens and mound crab meat on the greens. Combine mayonnaise, chili sauce, green pepper, onion, chopped parsley and cayenne. Spoon over crab meat. Garnish with crab legs, eggs, tomatoes, olives, parsley sprigs and lemon wedges.

» CRAB SALAD 2

Combine all ingredients in order. This mixture handsomely serves 4 to 6 and is a superb cold crab dish. It's astonishing that apple does not appear more often as an ingredient in crab salad recipes.

2 cups crab meat (back fin preferred)
4 tbsp. celery (including some tops), finely chopped
1 good-sized apple, finely chopped
2 tbsp. parsley, minced
1 tsp. Dijon mustard
1/2 cup mayonnaise, or to taste
1/2 tsp. Worcestershire sauce
Dash cayenne
White pepper
1/2 tbsp. lemon juice
2 eggs, hard-cooked and chopped

» MAINE CRAB SALAD

Here's a delightfully simple, easy-to-make crab salad.

Remove any shell or cartilage from crab meat, being careful not to break the meat into small pieces. Combine all ingredients except lettuce. Chill. Serve on lettuce. Serves 6.

(From Maine Department of Marine Resources.)

1 lb. crab meat
1/2 cup mayonnaise or salad dressing
2 tbsp. chopped onion
Lettuce
2 tbsp. chopped sweet pickle
2 hard-cooked eggs, chopped
1/2 tsp. salt
Dash pepper

» CRAB-HAZELNUT SALAD

Here's a novel idea: put a hazelnut dressing on crab salad. Of course, you could use other nuts and nut oils, if you happen to have them, but we credit this recipe to the Oregon Hazelnut Marketing Board working with the Oregon Dungeness Crab Commission.

For the salad:

1 1/4 lb. crab meat
Curly endive (small quantity)
6 sprigs watercress
Green leaf and/or red leaf lettuce
   for 6 servings
Radicchio (small quantity)
1/4 cup roasted and chopped
   hazelnuts
3 hard-cooked eggs, quartered

For the dressing:

2 tbsp. white wine vinegar
1 tbsp. pear or apple brandy
3/8 cup hazelnut oil
Grated nutmeg
1 tbsp. Dijon mustard
2 tbsp. finely chopped tarragon
Pinch each salt, sugar, fresh
   ground pepper

In a large bowl, combine the vinegar, mustard, salt, sugar and pepper. Beat with a wire whisk. Add the nutmeg, tarragon and brandy. Beat well for 1 minute. Slowly add the oil in tiny droplets, beating constantly with the whisk. Taste for seasoning.

Just before serving, add the greens. Toss to coat the greens. Transfer to serving plates. Then divide the crab meat among the plates and sprinkle with hazelnuts. Garnish with egg. Serves 6.

CRAB SOUPS

For many years we pursued crab soups up and down the East Coast, from lowly small-town luncheonettes to elegant waterfront and city restaurants. We've spooned through hundreds of sad bowlfuls, only rarely finding a really excellent concoction.

The variety most often served in the East is really a vegetable soup with a bit of crab tossed in. The tastiness of the product depends on how good the vegetable soup was to begin with. To us, this type has always been disappointing.

Deciding that we prefer a creamy crab soup, we've downed many miserably floury mixtures masquerading as crab bisque, and we have found some good ones. But the queen of all crab soups, we think, is she-crab soup. And among those, the creation we like best is by Henry's restaurant in Charleston, S.C. After eating Henry's soup for four days and raving about its quality, we were given a nugget of knowledge by the niece of the Henry who started the restaurant. The basic seasoning, she said, is mace and sherry wine.

Back home, we began creating beautiful soups, always including mace and sherry. Mace! What a word—what a spice! Not a club, nor the spray used to disperse unruly mobs, but a deliciously aromatic spice. It's similar to, but more flavorful than, nutmeg. Mace is ground from the layer between the nutmeg shell and the outer husk. For us, it is the perfect accent for crab soup. Sherry for crab soup-making should be dry. If marsala is all you happen to have, it will do, but use less because it is sweet.

Here are two crab soup recipes, one which assumes you have lots of time to cook, and the second assuming you got home at the last minute for food preparation.

» CRAB SOUP 1

3 tbsp. celery (including some
   tops), finely minced
1 shallot or scallion, finely
   minced
1 cup water
1 1/2 cups crab meat (claw and
   body)
2 cubes chicken stock
2 eggs, hard-cooked*
1/4 tsp. mace
Dash garlic powder (optional)
2 tbsp. parsley stems, finely
   minced
1/4 lb. mushrooms, cut up
5 tbsp. margarine
3 1/2 tbsp. flour
3 1/2 cups milk
1/2 tsp. salt
Dash cayenne
1/3 cup sherry
Dash white pepper
Fresh parsley, finely minced

* If you prefer less cholesterol, use
1 yolk and 2 whites.

While the eggs are cooking, melt 1 1/2 tablespoons margarine in a small, heavy saucepan. Add very finely minced celery, parsley stems, shallot and mushrooms. On medium heat, toss frequently for 3 minutes. Add 1 cup water, cover, simmer 3 to 5 minutes and set aside.

Heat milk and chicken stock to boiling. Meanwhile, melt remaining 3 1/2 tablespoons margarine in a very heavy pot (we find the best is enamelled iron) and add flour. Mix with a wooden spoon on low heat for 2 to 3 minutes. Mixture will be frothy and bubbly. Add the hot milk and chicken stock mixture at once, stirring vigorously with a wire whisk so there won't be any lumps. Keep heat very low. Mash egg yolks well; mince whites. Add them and the celery mixture to the soup. Stir. Add the spices, sherry and crab. Stir carefully; simmer 20 minutes and taste.

This is where you're on your own. If you wish, you can add minute amounts of spices; as we said, this is the ad-lib school of cooking, and only you know what pleases your palate. But remember, crab can be overwhelmed easily by too-strident spicing.

Serve soup in warm bowls with freshly minced parsley on top. Crackers or melba toast are good accompaniments. With a large, tossed vegetable salad and some fruit for dessert, this is a deliciously satisfying meal for 4, or it makes a delightful first course for 6 to 8.

» CRAB SOUP 2

This is the jiffy soup. Start cooking the eggs as soon as you arrive in the kitchen; hard-cooking them takes longer than anything else in the recipe.

2 eggs, hard-cooked
1 can cream of celery or cream of
    chicken soup
1/4 soup can sherry
Dash cayenne
Dash garlic powder
1 tsp. dehydrated onion flakes
1 can cream of mushroom soup
1 3/4 soup cans milk
1/4 tsp. mace
Dash white pepper
1 1/2 cups crab meat (claw and
    body)

Use a heavy-bottomed pot (enamelled iron is best) and mix soups, milk and sherry with wire whisk. Add spices and crab meat. When soup mixture is smooth and hot, mash hard-cooked egg yolks and chop whites finely and add both to soup. Taste before you add salt, since there is usually enough salt in the canned soups. Keep heat low, so soup warms slowly and flavors have a chance to blend. Let soup simmer while you make salad.

You will find out by experimenting which canned product makes the best crab soup. We generally use Campbell's with reduced sodium. Serves 4 to 6.

» SHE-CRAB SOUP

In our kitchen we have a colorful little poster from Charleston, South Carolina, with this recipe for she-crab soup.

(**Note**: This recipe should tell you to blend the butter and flour until they are foaming and heat the milk before adding. Also, unless you live where you can get crab roe, use two mashed, hard-cooked egg yolks as a substitute.)

Melt butter and blend in flour. Add milk, crab meat, roe and all seasonings except sherry. Cook slowly over hot water for 20 minutes. Add 1/2 table-spoon warmed sherry to individual soup bowls. Add soup and top each serving with whipped cream. Serve hot. Serves 4 as a main course; 6 to 8 as a first course.

2 cups white crab meat and crab roe
1 quart milk
1/4 pint cream (whipped)
Salt and pepper
1/2 tsp. Worcestershire sauce
A few drops onion juice
1/4 lb. butter
1/4 tsp. mace
1 tbsp. flour
4 tbsp. dry sherry

» CURRIED CRAB SOUP

1/2 lb. crab meat
4 tbsp. margarine
1/2 cup finely chopped onion
1 clove minced garlic
1/2 cup peeled, diced apple
2 tsp. flour
1 tbsp. curry powder
1/2 cup peeled, chopped tomato
3 cups chicken broth
1/2 cup heavy cream
1/2 tsp. each, salt and pepper
1/4 tsp. liquid hot pepper sauce

Sauté onion and garlic in margarine until tender. Add apple and stir. Sprinkle in flour and curry powder. Add tomato and chicken broth and stir rapidly with a wire whisk. When thick and smooth, add cream, salt, pepper and pepper sauce. Then gently fold in crab meat and heat thoroughly. Serves 4.

(From a recipe published by Texas A & M University.)

» CRAB BISQUE 1

We think that crabs in almost any form are food fit for a king, but we have only recently learned that presidents favored them, too. Both George Washington and Franklin Delano Roosevelt liked to eat crab bisque. Here are a couple of recipes for that lovely soup. First, the low-calorie version.

Heat stock and milk to boiling with celery, onion, cloves and bay leaf. Simmer for about 15 minutes. Strain. Melt margarine and stir in flour with wire whisk for about 4 to 5 minutes, until frothy. Add hot milk mixture and crab meat. Add salt and Tabasco. Simmer slowly, stirring carefully. Serve in hot bowls; garnish with parsley.
Serves 4 to 6.

3 cups milk
1 small onion, chopped
2 cloves
1 tbsp. margarine
1/4 tsp. salt
1 1/2 cups crab meat
1 stalk celery, chopped
1/2 cup (4 cubes) chicken stock
1 tbsp. flour
1 bay leaf
1/2 tsp. Tabasco
Fresh parsley, finely minced

» CRAB BISQUE 2

The second crab bisque recipe makes a much more delicious and, alas, much richer soup. There are happy mediums that a resourceful cook can concoct. Our motto: Taste frequently while preparing and add seasonings in small amounts.

1/2 cup mushrooms, sliced
1/2 cup celery, finely chopped
3 tbsp. butter
1 tbsp. flour
2 hard-cooked eggs, sieved
Grated peel of 1 lemon
1 tsp. Worcestershire sauce
1/2 cup heavy cream
1 quart milk
1 tsp. onion juice
1/4 tsp. mace
Salt and pepper to taste
2 cups crab meat
1/4 cup sherry

Sauté mushrooms and chopped celery lightly in 1 tablespoon butter. Cover, simmer and set aside. Blend 2 tablespoons melted butter, flour, sieved eggs, lemon peel and Worcestershire sauce to a paste and put into very heavy pot (or top of double boiler). Scald milk and cream together; blend in onion juice and mace. Using wire whisk, stir into paste in heavy pot. Bring to boiling, stirring constantly. Add crab meat, sautéed celery and mushrooms and sherry. Heat slowly so that all flavors blend.
Serves 4 to 6.

» CRAB BISQUE 3

Heat the milk and butter in a saucepan and add all the seasonings. Dissolve the cornstarch in the half-and-half, and when the seasoned milk and butter mix has come almost to a boil, stir it in and cook until the bisque thickens. Add sherry and crab and serve hot. Makes two quarts.

There are other crab bisque recipes that call for dismembering live, uncooked crabs. We reject those.

1 lb. crab meat
2 quarts milk
1/4 cup half-and-half
1/4 cup butter
1 tsp. dry mustard
1/2 tsp. white pepper
1/4 cup cornstarch
4 cubes chicken stock
3 ounces dry sherry
1 tbsp. Old Bay seasoning
1 tsp. celery salt
Dash of Worcestershire sauce

CRABS PLUS OTHER SEAFOOD

Here are ways to combine crab with other seafood—one in a bisque, another in a big stew that could be called a bouillabaisse. You could call it gumbo if you add okra, as we did in the third recipe.

» SEAFOOD BISQUE

1 lb. crab meat (or surimi)
1/2 lb. sea scallops, rinsed and cut
    into bite-sized pieces
8 cups skim milk
1/2 cup flour
1/2 cup minced celery
1/2 tsp. white pepper
1/2 cup dry sherry
1/2 cup margarine
1/2 cup minced fresh onions
2 cubes chicken stock
2 stalks fresh parsley (or 1 tsp.
    parsley flakes)
1/2 tsp. salt

Melt the margarine in a 5-quart heavy pot and sauté the onions and celery 2 minutes. Blend in the flour and seasonings. Gradually add the skim milk, stirring constantly over medium heat for about 10 minutes, until it thickens, without boiling. Add the seafood and sherry and heat for 5 minutes, again without boiling. Serves 8 to 10.

» SEAFOOD SUPREME

Melt margarine in large soup pot. Add onions, green peppers and celery and sauté until tender. Add flour and blend well. Add tomatoes, bring to a boil and simmer for 20 minutes. Then add the seafood and all seasonings except the thickener and simmer another 20 minutes. Finally, add the thickener and simmer 3 more minutes. Sprinkle with green onions and serve with cooked rice. Makes 1/2 gallon or 10 to 12 servings.

(Adapted from a bulletin of the Florida Department of Agriculture and Consumer Services.)

1 pint oysters, undrained
1 lb. fish fillets, cut into 3-inch
   pieces
1 lb. crab meat
1 lb. shrimp, peeled and deveined
1/4 cup margarine or butter
1 cup chopped onions
1 cup chopped green peppers
1 cup chopped celery
1/2 cup all-purpose flour
4 16-oz. cans tomatoes,
   undrained
2 tsp. granulated garlic
1 tsp. cumin
1 tsp. crushed red pepper
1 tsp. oregano
1 tsp. basil
1 tsp. thyme
2 tsp. file (thickener)*
1/2 cup thinly sliced green onions
4 cups cooked rice

* Another thickener, such as cornstarch, can be used. File, made from ground sassafras leaves, is a thickener and flavoring used in Creole dishes, such as gumbo.

» SEAFOOD GUMBO

1/2 lb. raw, peeled and deveined
  shrimp (fresh or frozen)
1/2 lb. crab meat, fresh, frozen or
  canned
1/2 cup chopped celery
2 cups sliced fresh okra or 10 ounces
  frozen okra, sliced
1/4 tsp. sugar
1 whole bay leaf
2 lbs. canned tomatoes
1/3 cup butter or other spread
2/3 cup chopped green onion and
  tops
2 cloves garlic, finely chopped
1 1/2 tsp. salt
1/2 tsp. pepper
1/4 tsp. crushed whole thyme
6 drops liquid hot pepper sauce
1 1/2 cups cooked rice

Stove Top Directions:
Cook rice according to package directions. Put butter, onion, garlic, celery, okra and seasonings in a soup pot and sauté until tender. Add tomatoes, bring to a boil and simmer 20 minutes. Add seafood and simmer another 20 minutes. Serves 6.

Microwave Directions:
Thaw frozen seafood. Remove all shell or cartilage from crab. Combine butter, onion, garlic, celery, okra and seasonings in a 3-quart bowl. Cover. Cook 12 minutes on Medium, stirring occasionally to separate okra. Add tomatoes and seafood. Re-cover. Cook 16 minutes on Medium, stirring occasionally. Remove bay leaf. Place 1/4 cup rice in each of six soup bowls. Fill with gumbo. Serves 6.

(Adapted from a recipe of the Florida Department of Agriculture and Consumer Services.)

» BAKED OYSTERS AND CRAB

Those who love oysters can combine the delicate flavors of oysters and crab in this gourmet dish from the Florida Department of Agriculture and Consumer Services. It can be served as an appetizer or an entrée.

Wash oysters thoroughly. Shuck and place oysters on deep half of shell, after removing any remaining shell particles. Arrange oysters on baking sheet and set aside. Combine crab meat with remaining ingredients; mix well. Top each oyster with 1 teaspoon of mixture and bake in preheated oven at 450° F for 10 minutes or until edges curl. Serves 6.

36 oysters in the shell
1 lb. crab meat
1/4 cup finely chopped onions
2 tbsp. white wine or sherry
10 ounces low-fat Swiss cheese, grated

CRAB ENTRÉES

» BEULAH'S CRAB IMPERIAL

We found the following recipe in a small cookbook called *Meal-time Magic*, compiled years ago by the children in the remarkable little elementary school our children attended in the Village of Arden, Delaware. Beulah told us this is a very old, authentic Baltimore recipe which she liked because it is simple and does not attempt to "enhance" the crab. She quoted Mrs. Millard Tawes, wife of a former Maryland governor, who firmly believed that "crab cannot be enhanced—only complemented."

You will note that this recipe does not contain green pepper, which is in most Imperial recipes. You may add some, finely minced, if you like. Beulah preferred to omit it, and so do we.

1 lb. crab meat (back fin)
1 tsp. prepared mustard
1/8 lb. butter
2 1/2 tbsp. mayonnaise
1 egg, beaten
Chopped parsley (optional)
Lemon juice (optional)
Buttered bread crumbs

Mix mustard, butter, mayonnaise and egg together and combine with crab meat. Place in casserole. Sprinkle buttered crumbs on top. Bake for 30 minutes at 350° F. Serves 3 or 4.

» RHODA'S CRAB

We asked our friend and longtime neighbor Jean Brachman, who is a wizard of a cook, to share a favorite crab recipe with us. She responded with this member of the Crab Imperial family, a recipe supplied by her friend Rhoda, who earns a culinary crown with this entry.

Set oven at 375° F. Combine all but the last three ingredients. Rub the butter into the crumbs with your fingers. Set aside. Divide the crab mixture into 8 shells. Top with buttered bread crumbs. Sprinkle with paprika. Bake 15 minutes until bubbly. Serves 4.

1 lb. crab meat (back fin)
1/2 green pepper, chopped
1/2 pimento, chopped
1 tbsp. lemon juice
1 tsp. Worcestershire sauce
1/2 cup mayonnaise
3 drops Tabasco
1/2 tsp. dry mustard
1/4 tsp. salt
1/4 tsp. white pepper
4 tbsp. fine bread crumbs
2 tbsp. butter
Paprika

» TEXAS CRAB CASSEROLE

1 lb. crab meat

1 egg, beaten

1/2 cup chopped onion

2 slices bacon

1/2 cup chopped celery

1 clove minced garlic

1 1/2 cups cracker crumbs

1/4 cup milk

1/2 cup melted margarine

2 tbsp. chopped parsley

2 tsp. dry mustard

1/2 tsp. salt

1 tsp. Worcestershire sauce

Dash cayenne pepper

Stove Top Directions:

Cook bacon until crisp. Dry it with paper towels, then crumble it and set it aside. Sauté vegetables in bacon fat. Then combine all ingredients in a mixing bowl and mix well. Transfer to a casserole. Bake at 350° F for 25 minutes. Serves 6.

Microwave Directions:

Prepare as with stove top cooking. Place in microwave-safe casserole. Cook on High 12 minutes. Serves 6.

(Based on a recipe from Texas A & M University.)

» LAST-MINUTE CRAB CASSEROLE

When you have some crab meat in the refrigerator, but get home too late to be as elaborate about dinner as you had planned, here's a tasty, easy solution to the problem of what to serve 6 people.

Heat oven to 350° F. Rub casserole or shells with margarine. Heat the soup and add the chicken cubes, milk and vermouth. Add the crab meat, uncooked peas and cayenne. Taste before adding salt or additional seasoning. Place in the casserole or individual shells and top with grated cheese. Sprinkle paprika over all. Bake about 20 minutes until lightly browned.

1 can condensed cream of mushroom soup
2 cubes chicken stock
1/2 soup can milk
1 tbsp. vermouth
1 lb. crab meat
1 package frozen peas, uncooked
Dash cayenne
Salt
1/2 cup Swiss cheese, grated
Paprika

» CRAB QUICHE

1 1/2 cups crab meat

1 tbsp. celery, finely chopped

1 tbsp. scallion, finely chopped

2 tbsp. parsley (including stems), finely chopped

3 tbsp. sherry

Pastry for 9-inch pie shell or frozen pie shell

4 eggs, beaten

1 cup milk

1 cup light cream

1/4 tsp. mace

1/2 tsp. salt

1/4 tsp. white pepper

Try to make sure the crab meat is free of shell and cartilage. (Go ahead, try!) Put the first four ingredients in the sherry and refrigerate 1 hour. Heat oven to 450° F. Bake the pastry shell for 5 minutes. Put the crab meat mixture evenly in the pie shell. Combine the rest of the ingredients and add to the pie shell. Bake for 15 minutes at 450° F; reduce heat to 350° F and bake about 10 minutes more (or until a knife inserted one inch from edge of shell comes out clean). Serve small pieces as an hors d'oeuvre or larger slices as a main luncheon course for 6.

» CRAB MORNAY

Melt butter in a heavy pan; add flour and stir on low heat for several minutes. Heat milk, vermouth and stock to boiling; add all at once to the roux and stir with a wire whisk until smooth. This will take several minutes. Add the grated cheeses, continuing to stir with whisk until sauce is completely smooth. Add crab meat and stir gently on low heat. Taste and add spices.

Put in shells, ramekins or casserole and sprinkle buttered crumbs on top. Bake at 350° F about 15 minutes or until bubbly and light brown. Garnish with crisp parsley. Serves 4.

2 tbsp. butter or margarine
3 tbsp. flour
1 1/2 cups milk
1/4 cup dry vermouth
2 chicken stock cubes (or 1/4 cup stock or dehydrated chicken bouillon)
1/4 cup Parmesan cheese, grated
1/4 cup Swiss cheese, grated
1 lb. crab meat
Salt and white pepper
2 dashes mace
Buttered bread crumbs
Fresh parsley

» CRAB MEAT DEWEY

We've never heard whether this is named for the admiral or for the governor, but either way it makes a delicious entrée served with a tossed salad and fresh, buttered lima beans. If mushrooms are easily available and you need to stretch this recipe, feel free to increase their amount. Mushrooms and crab meat complement each other very well, their delicate flavors blending beautifully.

3/4 cup mushrooms, sliced to
   retain the mushroom shape
5 tbsp. margarine or butter
1 1/4 cups milk
2 cubes chicken stock
2 tbsp. dry vermouth
Dash mace
1 lb. crab meat, well picked over to
   remove cartilage
3 1/2 tbsp. flour
Salt and white pepper
1/4 cup light cream
Fresh parsley

Sauté mushrooms in 1 tablespoon margarine for a few minutes. Set aside. Heat milk, chicken stock and vermouth to boiling. Melt 2 tablespoons margarine and sauté crab meat for a few minutes, tossing constantly. In a heavy pot, melt 2 tablespoons margarine, add flour and stir on low heat until mixture is frothy (3 or 4 minutes). Add hot milk mixture to roux all at once, stirring constantly with wire whisk. When sauce has thickened, add crab meat and mushrooms. On low heat, reheat whole mixture, adding cream a little at a time. You may not need to use the entire amount. Add salt, white pepper and mace to taste. Let simmer for 10 to 15 minutes. Serve from large casserole or heated individual ramekins. Garnish with fresh parsley. Serves 4.

» CURRIED CRAB ALMONDINE

This is a deliciously tasty way to serve crab. We suggest you may want to add less curry than the recipe calls for until you have tasted it, to make sure it's right for you.

In a heavy pot, sauté onion, celery and apple in 3 tablespoons margarine until onion is translucent. Add less than 1 tablespoon more margarine, the curry and flour. With wooden spoon, stir on medium low heat for at least 3 minutes. Heat milk to boiling and add to curry mixture, stirring constantly with wire whisk until sauce thickens. Taste and add salt and pepper as needed. Let sauce simmer about 15 minutes, stirring only occasionally. You may need to add a little milk or cream to get the right consistency. Then add the crab meat and almonds. Reheat, stirring very carefully to keep the crab pieces from breaking up. (**Note:** You can make the curry sauce earlier in the day and heat it up before adding the crab and almonds.) Spoon into greased shells and put under the broiler for a couple of minutes. Serves 4.

1 lb. crab meat
4 tbsp. margarine or butter
2 tbsp. onion, finely minced (or 2 tsp. dehydrated onion)
1 medium apple, chopped
1/2 cup celery, finely chopped
1 tbsp. curry powder
2 tbsp. flour
1 1/2 cups milk
1/2 tsp. salt
Dash pepper
1/2 cup toasted slivered almonds

» LEMON-BUTTERED CRAB MEAT

1 lb. crab meat (lump, if possible)
1/2 lb. butter or margarine
Juice of 1 lemon, strained
Fresh parsley, chopped
4 lemon wedges

Heat the oven to 400° F. Grease 4 shells or other ovenproof individual casseroles. Carefully pick over the crab meat and divide it among the shells. Apportion the butter in dots on top of each. Sprinkle with the lemon juice. Put the shells on a cookie sheet and bake briefly in the hot oven. In about 6 minutes, they should be golden brown and ready to be topped with the parsley and lemon wedges and served. Serves 4.

» SAVORY MAINE CRAB

6 tbsp. butter or margarine
1/2 cup flour
3/4 tsp. salt
1/8 tsp. pepper
1/4 tsp. Worcestershire sauce
1 1/2 tsp. prepared mustard
1/2 tsp. prepared horseradish
1 1/2 cups milk
13 ounces (2 cans) crab meat
1 tbsp. lemon juice
2 sprigs parsley, chopped
1 cup soft bread crumbs

Melt 4 tablespoons butter in heavy saucepan. Blend in flour and seasonings. Gradually add milk and cook until thickened, stirring constantly. Remove from heat and add next three ingredients. Put in 8 small baking dishes (crab-shaped if possible) or 4 small ramekins. Melt remaining 2 tablespoons butter and mix with crumbs. Sprinkle on mixture in baking dishes. Bake at 400° F for 10 minutes, until hot and crumbs are browned.

(From Maine Department of Marine Resources.)

» SPICED CRAB CLAWS

Stove Top Directions:

In a saucepan, heat butter and all ingredients except crab, lemon juice and parsley, until butter has melted. Stir. Spread out the crab claws in a baking dish. Pour on the seasoned, warmed butter. Bake 20 minutes at 350° F. Add lemon juice and parsley. Serves 4.

Microwave Directions:

Put butter in 4-cup glass container; add garlic, green onions, thyme, oregano, tarragon, salt and pepper. Cook on High for 1 1/2 to 2 minutes until butter foams. Remove from oven. Skim off and discard foam. Arrange claws in a 13 x 9-inch baking dish, with thicker parts toward the sides. Cook on High 1 to 2 minutes. Remove from oven. Pour in the seasoned butter. Add lemon juice and parsley. Serves 4.

4 cooked claws of Stone, King or
*   Snow crab*
1 clove garlic, minced
3 green onions, minced
1/4 tsp. thyme
1/4 lb. butter or other spread
Salt and pepper to taste
2 tbsp. parsley
1/4 tsp. oregano
1/2 tsp. tarragon
2 tbsp. lemon juice

» DIPS FOR CRAB CLAWS

Many dips are recommended for crab claws. Although we generally prefer very mild flavorings with crabs, we sometimes dip Blue crab claws in seafood sauce consisting of ketchup and as much prepared horseradish as we like. Others prefer mustard-based sauces or a mayonnaise sauce. Here are four, including a honey mustard and a sweet and sour sauce, both from the Florida Department of Agriculture and Consumer Services, which recommends them for Stone crab claws.

Honey Mustard Sauce

1 cup mayonnaise
2 tbsp. honey
2 tbsp. prepared mustard
1/3 cup half-and-half or light
   cream
2 tsp. coriander

Combine all ingredients and stir briskly until blended.

Sweet and Sour Sauce

1/2 cup ketchup
3 tbsp. red wine vinegar
1 tbsp. lemon juice
1 tsp. horseradish
1/3 cup orange marmalade
1 tbsp. soy sauce
2 tsp. dry mustard
1/4 tsp. curry powder

Bring mixture to a boil in a saucepan. Reduce heat and cook for 1 minute, stirring constantly. Serve warm.

Mustard Sauce

Beat mustard and mayonnaise in a mixing bowl for 1 minute with an electric mixer on low speed, then stir in the other ingredients. Add more mustard if you want it spicier.

3 tsp. dry mustard
4 tbsp. milk or half-and-half
Pinch of salt
1 cup mayonnaise
2 1/2 tsp. Worcestershire sauce

Mayonnaise Dip

Here's a dip, easy to make, that adds delicate flavor to commercial mayonnaise. We use the low-fat variety. The dip is based on a recipe published by the Oregon Dungeness Crab Commission, which of course recommends it for the local crab, but it can be used with any crab meat.

Mix all ingredients in a blender or food processor.

1/3 cup spinach or sorrel
1 clove garlic
1 scallion
1 cup mayonnaise
1/2 cup olive oil

» CHARLESTON MEETING STREET CRAB MEAT

Our former summer neighbor and fellow crab devotée, Dot Shellender, shared this crab entrée with us. It's an interesting transplant from South Carolina.

4 tbsp. butter
4 tbsp. flour
1/2 pint cream
Salt and pepper
4 tbsp. sherry
1 lb. crab meat
3/4 cup sharp provolone cheese, grated

Melt butter and blend in flour over low heat. Remove pan from heat. Heat cream and slowly add to butter mixture until smooth. Return to heat and cook slowly until sauce is thickened. Season to taste with salt and pepper. Remove from heat and add sherry and crab meat. Pour mixture into a buttered casserole or individual baking dishes. Sprinkle with grated cheese and bake in a 350° F oven, uncovered, for 20 to 25 minutes. Serves 4.

» CRAB CRÊPES

We first ate crab crêpes in a little French restaurant in New York, where they were served rolled up as a first course or extended into a *gâteau* as an entrée. We were delighted with the idea of wedding crab to crêpe, and we tried several variations at home. Now that crêpes are "in" and even the biscuit mix makers have a recipe on their packages for making crêpes, we recalled the enchanting *gâteau*.

We don't give the basic crêpe recipe here—those thin pancakes are simple to produce and it's easy to find directions. Maybe you even have one of those fancy crêpe makers. So, make some crêpes and try crab as a new filling. Any of the creamed crab recipes will do nicely—Newburg, Mornay, Last-Minute Crab Casserole. Make the sauce thick. Save some of the crab mixture after you have filled the crêpes, and thin it down to use over them.

If you want to serve rolled crêpes, spoon some crab filling on the crêpe and roll it up. Sauté lightly in butter or margarine, and spoon more of the same crab filling, thinned down, on top.

To make a layer cake or *gâteau*, here's the procedure. Lightly grease a baking pan. Put one crêpe in, then spoon on some crab filling. Put another crêpe on top, and again add filling. Use four crêpes for each *gâteau*, ending with a crêpe on top. Ladle sauce over the whole thing.

You can make the crêpes and the filling in the morning and make the *gâteau* about a half hour before serving. Warm the sauce and assemble the *gâteau*. Put in a 350° F oven to heat through. Try sprinkling the top with a little grated cheese before the oven warming. Use pimento or parsley as a garnish.

Don't be afraid to try variations. If mushrooms are plentiful, add some to the sauce. Or make a vari-layered *gâteau* by using the crab mixture for one layer, mushrooms for another. Or make a Florentine mound, using spinach for the bottom layer.

Better yet, invent your own crab-layered crêpes.

» CRAB-STUFFED TOMATOES

Here's an exception to our aversion to the tomato-crab combination. It relies on both the tomatoes and crab meat being sweet and lovely, as both are when freshly picked.

6 large fresh tomatoes
Salt and pepper
3 tbsp. butter or margarine
1/4 cup fresh parsley, minced
2 tbsp. scallion, minced
1 lb. crab meat
1 tbsp. lemon juice
1 tbsp. dry vermouth (optional)
1/4 cup grated Swiss cheese
1/4 cup fine bread crumbs

Remove the stem ends and centers with seeds from the tomatoes, and sprinkle with salt and pepper. Melt the butter and add to it the parsley, scallion, crab meat, lemon juice and vermouth. Mix carefully to blend, but try not to break up the crab meat. Put crab mixture in the tomatoes, then place tomatoes in a greased shallow baking dish. Combine the cheese and bread crumbs and sprinkle the tops of the tomatoes with the mixture. Bake for about 20 minutes in a 350° F oven. Serves 6.

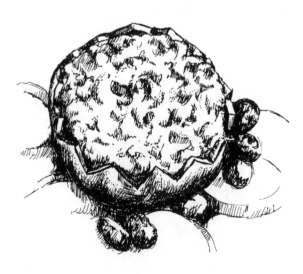

» OPEN-FACE CRAB MEAT AND CHEESE SANDWICH

This is another treasure from our neighbor Dot's collection. This recipe will serve a gem of a lunch for six.

Blend the first five ingredients, after picking over crab meat to remove bits of cartilage and shell. Cut 6 of the slices of toast in half diagonally. Spread tartar sauce on all of the toast. Place toast on a cookie sheet, arranged into 6 servings—1 whole slice of toast flanked by 2 triangles. Spread the crab mixture so that toast is covered; add a slice of cheese to each serving. Sprinkle the tops with paprika and put under broiler until bubbly.

Prepare for the enhancement of your reputation as an inventive cook, as your guests spread reports of this tasty luncheon.

1 lb. crab meat (back fin preferred)
Dash Tabasco
1 tsp. Worcestershire sauce
1 tsp. lemon juice
1/4 cup mayonnaise
12 slices white bread, toasted
12 slices American cheese
5 tbsp. tartar sauce
Paprika

» GINNY'S CRAB SANDWICH

Cheese goes well with crab, and this recipe is a convenient vehicle for a lunch featuring crab meat. It's a second sandwich recipe—this time from our daughter-in-law, Virginia.

8 ounces crab meat
4 ounces any soft cheese with garlic
2 tbsp. grated Parmesan cheese
1/4 cup celery, diced
2 tbsp. green onion, minced
2 tbsp. lemon juice
Dash pepper
6 bagels or buns or 12 pieces of
*   toast*
2 tbsp. capers, drained
2 tbsp. low-fat mayonnaise

Combine all ingredients except the bread in a bowl and mix. Slice the bagels or buns in half horizontally. Spread about 1/4 cup of the mixture on 6 halves of the buns or bagels or 6 slices of toast; cover with the matching pieces. Fold a paper towel around each sandwich, and put all 6 on a plate. Microwave on High 2 1/2 minutes, or warm in conventional oven.

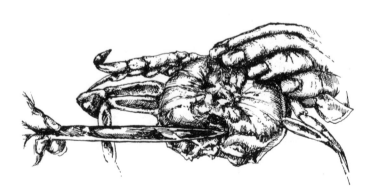

» STUFFED AVOCADOS

Remove any shell or cartilage from the crab meat, which can be of any kind, and may include surimi. Melt butter and blend in flour. Add milk gradually and cook until thick and smooth, stirring constantly. Add seasonings, pimento, olives and crab.

Cut avocados in half; remove seed. Fill centers with crab mixture. Sprinkle cheese over top of each. Place in a greased baking pan. Bake in moderate oven at 350° F for 20 to 25 minutes until brown. Serves 6.

(This recipe was adapted from a leaflet of the Virginia Institute of Marine Science.)

1 lb. crab meat
2 tbsp. butter or other spread
2 tbsp. flour
1 cup milk
1/4 tsp. salt
Dash pepper
1/4 tsp. Worcestershire sauce
2 tbsp. chopped pimento
2 tbsp. chopped olives
3 ripe avocados
1/4 cup grated cheese

» CRAB PIZZA

Pizza can be found with a broad variety of toppings—why not crab? The Florida Department of Agriculture and Consumer Services, which contains the Bureau of Seafood and Aquaculture, came up with this one.

1 lb. crab meat
1 container (8 oz.) green onion dip
1 large pre-cooked gourmet pizza
  crust
1/2 cup sliced ripe olives
1 package (8 oz.) shredded
  mozzarella cheese

Place pizza crust on pizza pan or cookie sheet. Spread dip evenly on pizza crust, leaving 1/2 inch around edges.

Arrange crab meat evenly on top of onion dip. Sprinkle with black olives and cheese. Bake at 450° F for 10 minutes or until hot. Serves 6.

SOFT SHELLS

The Blue crab in its soft shell state is highly regarded as a delicacy in the East. They're easy to sauté, deep fat fry or broil, and we give directions for cooking them on an outdoor grill. We strongly recommend sautéing. If you catch the crabs or buy them live, you have to clean them before cooking. The frozen ones you buy are already cleaned.

To clean the live crab, first cut off the protrusion at the front center, between the claws. It's what passes for the head on a crab, and it can easily be cut with scissors or a knife. Then lift the tips of the soft shell and scrape out the "devil's fingers," as you do with steamed hard shells. Finally, pull off the apron on the bottom and remove the spongy parts. The remaining shell is good to eat, along with the meat.

» LIBBY'S SAUTÉED SOFT SHELLS

Without doubt, this is the simplest and tastiest way to cook soft shells. They may be fried in deep fat after being dipped in eggs and crumbs, if you prefer, but we think that hides the delicacy of the crab flavor.

Soft shells are delicious cooked under the broiler, although that means having to baste them and heating up the kitchen.

1 dozen soft shell crabs
Flour
Salt and pepper
Butter and oil (we use corn oil)
Minced parsley
Lemon wedges

Dry the clean soft shells on paper towels. Dredge them with the flour, seasoned with salt and pepper. Shake them so that the flour coating is very light. Heat the butter and oil together in a heavy skillet. Sauté the soft shells until they are light brown and crisp, turning to get both sides done. Remove to a hot platter, top with minced parsley and serve with lemon wedges. This will make 4 to 6 servings, depending on the size of the crabs and the appetite of the diners.

» LEMON-BASIL-BUTTER SAUCE

Another good way to serve soft shells is with a sauce. First, mix 1 tablespoon Old Bay seasoning with 3/4 cup flour before dredging the crabs. Then sauté them, as directed in Libby's recipe on the previous page. Heat 4 ounces of butter with the juice of 1 lemon and 1/4 bunch fresh basil or 1 tablespoon dried basil leaves. Pour over the cooked crabs.

There are exceptions to most rules, and our rule on always sautéing soft shells gave way to "almost always" when, in the course of doing some pleasurable research for this edition, we tested the buttermilk-battered soft shells at Harry's Savoy Grill, north of Wilmington, Delaware. They were superb. Executive Chef David Banks provided the recipe created by Chef Joseph Misero III, and added one by Chef Corey L. Waters for crab fritters.

» BUTTERMILK-BATTERED SOFT SHELL CRABS

12 jumbo soft shell crabs, cleaned

10 cups seasoned flour*

3 cups buttermilk

3 cups whole milk

Peanut oil for frying

*   Seasoned flour:
Sift together: 9 cups all-purpose flour, 1 cup cornstarch, 2 tbsp. salt, 1 tbsp. white pepper, 2 tbsp. garlic powder and 2 tbsp. onion powder.

Put the seasoned flour and 6 cups milk in separate bowls. Dredge the soft shells first in the flour, then in the milk mixture, and then again in the flour, coating the crab completely each time. Deep fry crabs upside-down in peanut oil at 350° F until the legs curl upwards out of the oil (about 90 seconds). Turn the crabs and cook for another 90 seconds. Serve with Lemon Beurre Blanc** and garnish with chives. Serves 6.

2 cups white wine

1 tbsp. chopped shallots

1 bay leaf

9 ounces whole butter, cut into cubes

1 sprig fresh thyme

10 whole black peppercorns

3/4 cup heavy cream

2 tbsp. fresh lemon juice

** Lemon Beurre Blanc
Combine wine, thyme, shallots, peppercorns and bay leaf in saucepan. Heat over medium heat and reduce until nearly dry. Add cream and heat until thickened. Over low heat, slowly whisk in butter cubes until all butter is melted and sauce is creamy. Keep sauce above room temperature, but *do not let boil*. Add lemon juice and strain.

» SOFT SHELL CRAB FRITTERS

Wrap each soft shell half with a slice of zucchini. Place the following in three separate bowls: (1) flour, (2) eggs with water to thin slightly and (3) cornmeal and bread crumbs, combined.

Dredge the soft shells first in flour, then in the egg mixture and last in the cornmeal mixture. Deep fry in peanut oil at 350° F until golden brown—about 3 minutes. Serve with your favorite dipping sauce. Serves 6, as an appetizer.

3 jumbo soft shell crabs, cleaned and cut in half
1 large zucchini, sliced thin lengthwise
1/2 cup bread crumbs
3 eggs
1/2 cup cornmeal
Flour
Peanut oil for frying

» SOFT SHELLS ON THE OUTDOOR GRILL

While soft shells, which are somewhat fragile, are usually sautéed gently (or fried), they can also be prepared on the outdoor grill. Phyllis Hisey of Culpeper, Virginia, sent the following directions:

Splash the crabs with fresh lemon juice while the coals get properly gray, then brush on a little melted butter, augmented with 1/2 teaspoon of Tabasco. Put them on the grill; they will steam inside, while the outside turns crisp and crunchy. They are done when they feel firm to the spatula and the shell is a deep reddish-brown—8 to 10 minutes on each side.

Phyllis adds this warning: "Allow at least three crabs per person to avoid a riot."

» BREADED SOFT SHELLS

Some crab admirers like their soft shells fried and some like them both breaded and fried. We do not (ours are sautéed). But here's a recipe from a reliable source: the Virginia Institute of Marine Science.

12 soft crabs
1/4 cup milk
2 tsp. salt
2 eggs, beaten
3/4 cup flour
3/4 cup dry bread crumbs
Cayenne pepper and garlic to taste

Rinse crabs in cold water; drain. Combine eggs, salt and milk. Mix flour with crumbs. Dip crabs in egg mixture and then roll them in the flour and crumb mixture. If you want a heavy breading, let crabs sit for a few minutes, then repeat the dipping and rolling. The breaded crabs may be pan-fried or deep fat fried. For stronger flavoring, add cayenne pepper and garlic. Serves 6.

» SOFT SHELLS WITH PASTA

Soft shells are often savored alone, but they can be used as the crab meat in a dish with many ingredients, as illustrated by this entree prized by Jo Loria of Sarasota, Florida, who sometimes uses surimi instead of the soft shells.

Bring 6 quarts water to boil in large pot; add 2 tablespoons salt. Add the crab pieces and continue cooking until crabs are deep red and firm. Be careful not to break up the crabs with aggressive stirring. Add virgin olive oil. Add Anaheim peppers. Add the white wine and tomato sauce and reduce by half. Add escarole and cook another minute until escarole has wilted; remove from heat. Add onion and red jalapeños. Drop fusilli into boiling water and cook 7 to 9 minutes, or according to package instructions. Drain pasta in colander and pour hot pasta into pan with crabs. Return to medium heat and toss well to coat, about 1 minute. Pour onto warmed serving platter and serve immediately. Serves 4.

6 quarts water

2 tbsp. salt

6 soft shell crabs or 1 lb. surimi

6 tbsp. virgin olive oil

6 Anaheim peppers, cored, seeded and julienned

1 cup white wine

1 cup mild marinara sauce

2 cups escarole, finely chopped

1 medium red onion, thinly sliced

4 red jalapeños, cored, seeded and julienned

1 lb. fusilli bucati (or other pasta)

DEVILED CRABS

Many poor imitations are passed off in restaurants as "deviled crabs" and "crab cakes," while they don't taste much like crab for the simple reason that they don't have enough crab meat in them. They're often overloaded with bread crumbs, and they have given these dishes a bad name with many consumers. Of course, both deviled crabs and crab cakes can be made properly—if you put in enough crab meat to impart the crab flavor. Here are two good varieties of deviled crabs. The first is an unusual one from New Orleans, featuring a little brandy, and the second is a traditional one from Maryland.

» DEVILED CRABS LOUISIANA

1/2 cup shallots (or scallions)
Butter
1/4 cup brandy
1/2 tbsp. Dijon mustard
Enough béchamel sauce to bind the crab meat—about 1 cup
1 lb. crab meat (body and claw)
Salt and white pepper to taste
1 cup seasoned bread crumbs

Sauté shallots in butter until they are transparent. Remove pan from fire and swirl with the brandy, adding a little of the mustard at a time. Add the béchamel gradually. (You'll have to judge the exact amount of béchamel sauce needed to bind the crab, so add it slowly.) Finally, combine crab meat with this mixture. Taste and add salt and white pepper, if needed. Pour mixture into cleaned crab shells and cover each shell with seasoned bread crumbs. Dot each shell with butter and put under broiler until crumbs brown. Serves 4 to 6, depending on size of shells.

Crab shells can be cleaned up easily and used as natural serving dishes for many crab concoctions. The advantage, as in using a ramekin or piece of pottery in the shape of a clam or crab shell, is that each individual serving is in its own neat container.

To transform those messy-looking shells into the most inexpensive ramekins, first scrub the shells well with a stiff brush. Then put them in a pot, add 1 tablespoon baking soda for each 6 shells, cover them with water and bring to a boil. Let simmer for 20 minutes. Dry the shells, and there are your new dishes. Keep them clean—treat them as you would any ramekin. The greatest advantage is the replacement cost.

» DEVILED CRABS MARYLAND

This recipe came from Annapolis. It has an unusual ingredient for this dish—sage.

3/4 cup milk
3 tbsp. margarine or butter
2 tbsp. celery, very finely minced
2 tbsp. onion, very finely chopped
   (try half this amount, if you like)
2 tbsp. flour
Dash lemon juice
1/2 tsp. dry mustard
1/2 tsp. sage
1 tsp. Worcestershire sauce
Dash cayenne
Salt and white pepper
1 egg, beaten
1 lb. crab meat (body and claw)
2 tbsp. parsley, minced
Buttered fine bread crumbs

Heat 1/2 cup milk while you sauté the onion and celery in margarine until they are translucent, but not brown. Blend in flour and stir on low heat until flour has a chance to cook a little. Mixture will be a little foamy. Add hot milk and stir with a wire whisk. Add the lemon juice and all seasoning except salt. Beat the egg in a bowl with 1/4 cup milk. Stir a little of the hot sauce into the egg and milk mixture; then add the mixture to the sauce in the pot. Add the crab meat and parsley. Taste and add salt if necessary. Reheat, stirring to blend well. Spoon into greased shells or ramekins and top with buttered crumbs. Bake in a 350°F oven for 15 to 20 minutes or until browned.

» QUICK TARTAR SAUCE

This is not very sophisticated, but it's still a fine accompaniment for deviled crab.

We don't give quantities, because this is a natural for ad-lib production. Start with the mayonnaise (about 1 cup), then add the onion, relish, Worcestershire sauce and olives with pimento, deciding as you go along how much of each component will make the sauce right for you. The sauce can be kept in a jar in the refrigerator if not used all at once. It is better when made early in the day you plan to use it, so that the flavors have time to blend.

Mayonnaise
Onion or scallion (mostly juice), very finely minced
Green pickle relish, well drained
Worcestershire sauce
Salad olives, well drained and chopped fine

CRAB CAKES

Despite the fact that many consumers love crab cakes, we usually find them dull and lacking in crab flavor. As a quick lunch at a restaurant, a crab cake sandwich is welcome, but it's rarely an adventure in tempting taste. Part of the problem is too high a ratio of filler to crab, and another part is overuse of the fat in which the cakes are fried. We suggest you avoid ordering them deep-fried if they are available pan-fried.

Crab cakes do not require lump meat; they can be made with claw meat, and a little dilution with surimi is acceptable. There are hundreds of variations on how to make crab cakes. Those that won a Maryland contest at which we were among the judges consisted of lump crab meat held together with a binder, such as low-fat mayonnaise, and not much else other than mild seasoning. We suggest you experiment with that type, or try the recipe for Lemon-Buttered Crab Meat (page 106), which is similar. And here are several recipes for more traditional crab cakes that are also very satisfactory.

» HARRY BECK'S CRAB CAKES

Our friend Harry Beck, of Dover, Delaware, an expert racing car mechanic, showed with this recipe that he also has expertise in the kitchen. His cakes are pleasantly moist and tasty.

Mix all ingredients together. Spoon into iron frying pan in which butter and oil have been heated. Brown only a few minutes on each side. Serves 6.

1 lb. crab meat

2 eggs, beaten

1/2 cup fine cracker crumbs

3 tbsp. mayonnaise

2 tbsp. onion, finely minced

1 tbsp. green pepper, finely minced

1 tsp. prepared mustard (we use Dijon)

Salt and pepper to taste

Butter and/or oil for pan frying

» ORIENTAL CRAB CAKES

1 lb. lump crab meat (or surimi)
2 jalapeño peppers, seeded and
    minced
1/4 cup chopped fresh basil
2 tsp. salt
2 eggs, beaten
2 tbsp. olive oil
2 cups basmati rice
1 tbsp. grated lemon peel
3 tbsp. chopped fresh mint
1/2 tsp. ground black pepper
1/4 cup dry bread crumbs

In a large bowl, mix the rice, jalapeños, lemon peel, basil and mint with the crab meat. Then add the salt, black pepper, eggs and bread crumbs. Form cakes about 2 inches in diameter, using about 1 tablespoon of the crab mixture for each.

Next, heat 1 tablespoon oil in a nonstick skillet and cook the cakes over medium heat 1 1/2 minutes per side until browned. Makes 12 cakes; serves 6.

» MARYLAND CRAB CAKES

1 lb. crab meat
1 cup Italian seasoned bread
    crumbs
1 large egg, beaten
1/4 cup low-fat mayonnaise
1/8 lb. butter
1 tsp. dry mustard
1 tsp. Worcestershire sauce
Salt and pepper to taste

Stove Top Directions:
In a bowl, mix bread crumbs, egg, mayonnaise and seasonings. Add crab meat and mix gently. Shape into 8 cakes. Pan-fry in butter on both sides. Serves 4.

Microwave Directions:
In a bowl, mix bread crumbs, egg, mayonnaise and seasonings. Add crab meat and mix gently. Shape into 8 cakes. Place 4 patties at a time in baking dish. Cover with waxed paper. Cook each batch on High 2 minutes, then turn and cook other side on High 2 minutes. Serves 4.

» AMY'S CRAB CAKES

Stove Top Directions:
Melt butter or margarine on low heat.
Pick crab carefully. Add bread crumbs,
minced pepper, sherry, salt, onion and
egg. On a plain plate or waxed paper,
combine bread crumbs and paprika.
Shape crab meat into 12 round patties.
Dip into butter and then into bread
crumb mixture. Pan-fry on both sides.
Serve with cocktail sauce. Serves 6.

16 ounces frozen crab meat
1 1/2 cups bread crumbs
1/4 cup minced red or green
  pepper
2 tbsp. minced onion
2 tsp. paprika
1 egg, beaten
1/4 cup sherry
1/2 tsp. salt
4 tbsp. butter or margarine
Cocktail sauce

Microwave Directions:
Pick crab carefully after thawing. Add
bread crumbs, minced pepper, sherry,
salt, onion and egg. On waxed paper,
combine bread crumbs and paprika.
Shape crab meat into 12 round patties.
Put butter in a baking dish. Cover with
a paper towel and heat on High for 1
minute or until melted. Dip the crab
patties in butter, then coat with bread
crumbs. Put half the crab cakes in the
baking dish. Cover with waxed paper.
Cook on High 3 to 5 minutes, until
cakes are set, turning once. Serve with
cocktail sauce. Serves 6.

CRAB NEWBURG

Crab Newburg is a classic seafood dish. We wondered for years where it got its name. Seeing it sometimes spelled "Newburgh," we thought that might be an affectation of elegance, or that the dish might be named for the city in New York. Now we've heard a story about the origin.

It seems that in New York City around the end of the last century, a gentleman named Wenburg dined frequently at a restaurant famous for its seafood dishes. He became a friend of the restaurateur who, when he created a new seafood concoction, honored one of his star customers by calling it Crab Wenberg. Later, the relationship between the two deteriorated, and the restaurateur changed the name to Newburg and deprived Mr. Wenburg of his place in the index of crab-meat cookery.

In preparing this dish, as well as others that require the addition of beaten egg yolks to the basic béchamel sauce, it is important to remember to beat the eggs with some cold milk, and then to add the hot cream sauce gradually, stirring all the while.

» CRAB NEWBURG 1

Heat 1 cup of milk to boiling. Melt butter in a very heavy pan, add flour and mix on low heat for 3 or 4 minutes, until frothy. Stirring with a wire whisk, add hot milk all at once. Continue stirring to ensure smoothness. Add paprika, salt, mace, cayenne and sherry. In mixing bowl, mix 1/2 cup cold milk with the beaten egg yolks. Slowly add the hot sauce to the egg mixture, stirring constantly with the whisk. Then put the sauce back in the pan. Add the crab meat and stir. Heat slowly and thoroughly. Serve on toast or in patty shells. Serves 4.

1/4 tsp. salt
Dash mace
Dash cayenne
1/2 cup sherry
3 egg yolks, beaten (or 1 yolk and
    2 whites)
1 lb. crab meat
1 1/2 cups milk (or milk and
    cream, or half-and-half)
2 1/2 tbsp. butter
3 tbsp. flour
1/2 tsp. paprika

» CRAB NEWBURG 2

4 tbsp. butter or margarine
1/2 cup fresh mushrooms, sliced
1 lb. crab meat
1/2 cup sherry, marsala or madeira
1 1/2 cups milk (or milk and
    cream, or half-and-half)
2 cubes chicken stock
3 tbsp. flour
1/4 tsp. mace
1/2 tsp. salt
2 tbsp. brandy
3 egg yolks, beaten

In 1 1/2 tablespoons butter, sauté mushrooms lightly and set aside. Put crab meat and sherry in a pan and heat slowly. Heat 1 cup milk with the chicken cubes. In a heavy pan, melt 2 1/2 tablespoons butter, add flour and stir for 2 or 3 minutes until frothy. Add the hot liquids and stir with a wire whisk; add mace and salt. To crab and sherry, add brandy and set aflame. When flame has died down, add the mushrooms. Now, add 1/2 cup cold milk to beaten eggs, beating with the whisk. Add a bit of the hot sauce, stir well and gradually add the rest of the hot mixture, stirring with the whisk all the while. Put back in the heavy pot. Add the crab and brandy mixture and heat slowly. Serve on toast or in patty shells. Serves 4.

MICROWAVE RECIPES

Here are five recipes for cooking crab in the microwave oven. The first four were adapted from recipes supplied by the Florida Department of Agriculture and Consumer Services.

» IMPERIAL WITH PINEAPPLE

Thaw crab if frozen. Combine crab, mayonnaise, pimento and seasonings. Mix well. Dip both sides of pineapple slices in 2/3 cup corn flake crumbs. Place in a baking dish. Place 1/6 of crab mixture on each slice. Sprinkle remaining crumbs over top of crab mixture. Heat, uncovered, 5 minutes on Medium or until mixture is hot.

1 lb. crab meat, fresh or frozen
1 tsp. chopped pimento
1/2 tsp. Worcestershire sauce
6 pineapple slices, drained
2/3 cup plus 1/4 cup fine corn flake crumbs
1/4 cup mayonnaise or salad dressing
1/2 tsp. salt
3 drops hot pepper sauce

» MICROWAVE CRAB QUICHE

1 lb. crab meat
1 cup grated Swiss cheese
3 eggs, slightly beaten
1 cup half-and-half
6 drops hot pepper sauce
Paprika
1 unbaked (deep dish) frozen pie
    shell
1 tsp. Worcestershire sauce
3/4 cup sliced ripe olives
1/4 cup chopped green onions
1/2 tsp. salt

Thaw crab meat if frozen. Thaw frozen pie shell to room temperature and transfer to a ceramic quiche dish or glass pie plate, pressing pastry firmly against sides to prevent shrinkage during cooking. Sprinkle Worcestershire sauce over crust; spread evenly with pastry brush. Prick pie crust with a fork several times. Microwave on High 3 minutes or until done. Let cool. Sprinkle cheese over bottom of pie shell. Add crab and olives. Mix eggs, half-and-half, onions, salt and pepper sauce and pour over crab and olives. Sprinkle with paprika. Microwave on High 15 minutes, rotating dish a quarter turn every 3 minutes. To test quiche for doneness, insert knife in center; quiche is "set" when knife comes out clean. Let stand for 2 minutes. May be served hot or at room temperature. Serves 6.

» HOT SHRIMP AND CRAB CASEROLE

Thaw seafood if frozen. Cut large shrimp in half. In a 1 1/2-quart shallow dish, combine celery and green pepper. Cook 3 minutes on High, or until tender. Add seafood, soup, water chestnuts, water, eggs, lemon juice and salt. Mix well. Cover. Cook 7 minutes on High or until shrimp are tender, stirring occasionally. Stir in stuffing mix. Sprinkle with cheese. Cook, uncovered, 3 minutes longer or until cheese melts. Serves 6.

1/2 lb. crab meat
1/2 lb. shrimp, peeled and
    deveined (fresh or frozen)
1 can (10 1/2 oz.) condensed
    cream of onion soup
1/2 cup sliced water chestnuts,
    drained
2 hard-cooked eggs, chopped
1 cup dry stuffing mix
3/4 cup chopped celery
1/4 cup chopped green pepper
1/4 cup water
1 tbsp. lemon juice
1/2 tsp. salt
1/2 cup shredded Cheddar cheese

» FESTIVE CRAB SPREAD

1 cup crab meat (fresh or canned)
8 ounces cream cheese
1 tbsp. milk
2 tsp. Worcestershire sauce
2 tbsp. chopped green onion
2 tbsp. toasted slivered almonds
Assorted crackers

In a mixing bowl, combine cream cheese, milk and Worcestershire sauce. Add crab meat and onion; blend well. Put mixture in an 8-inch pie plate. Top with almonds. Cook 2 minutes on High or until well heated. Serve warm with crackers. Makes about 2 cups of spread.

» FIESTA SHELLFISH

Put butter in a medium bowl. Cover with a paper towel and heat on High 1 minute or until melted. Add flour and salt and stir. Stir in sherry and half-and-half. Cook on High 3 to 4 minutes until the sauce thickens. Stir twice.

Place all the seafood except the crab claws in a 10-inch baking dish. Cook, covered, on High for 2 1/2 to 3 minutes, stirring once. Add sauce, pimentos, chopped parsley and crab claws. Cover and cook on High 1 1/2 to 2 minutes, just until the shrimp turn pink. Transfer to serving platter and add parsley garnish.

12 ounces frozen Snow or Stone crab claws
8 ounces sea scallops
8 ounces medium shrimp, peeled and deveined
2 tbsp. butter
1 tbsp. dry sherry
Parsley for garnish
2 tbsp. all-purpose flour
1/2 tsp. salt
10 ounces half-and-half
4 ounces pimentos
1 tbsp. chopped parsley

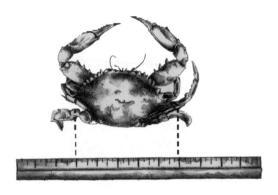

7 »«

A NOTE ON
NUTRITION

The Virginia Institute of Marine Science is one of our favorite authorities on seafood. A publication of the institute contained the following expert statement on "Seafood Nutrition—Fact and Fancy":

How many times have you heard that the fish is "brain food?" Or that eating oysters makes you more amorous?

The idea that eating fish enhances your brain dates back to the nineteenth century and a Harvard University scientist. He discovered that compounds containing phosphorus are abundant in the brain. So he urged people to eat fish, which is rich in phosphorus. The scientist reasoned that increased amounts of phosphorus in the brain would increase brain power—a concept that has since been disproved.

Oysters contain cholesterol, the basic building block for both male and female sex hormones. But the body produces enough cholesterol to satisfy our total needs. The additional cholesterol will not affect sexual behavior.

Seafood won't improve your IQ or act as a love potion. But it is high in protein and low in fat—a combination that makes seafood attractive to dieters. Many people have also learned that seafood is low in sodium and high in potassium. This combination is especially attractive to people with heart problems. Sodium causes the body to retain water and aggravates high blood pressure; potassium tends to negate the effects of sodium.

Part of developing a nutritional label for seafood involves determining if the nutrients present in fish are also available to the human body. The minerals in a food product may pass through the body instead of being used. For example, fish, which is considered a low moderate source of iron, is not a source of iron in the human body. But fish may help make the iron in other products available to humans. Seafoods may enhance the uptake of iron in foods such as spinach, wheat, and soybeans, which have iron normally not available to the human body. Similarly, the protein in fish helps enhance the availability of other minerals to the body.

The nutrients in seafood work in concert with the body and the other foods we consume. Fish has an important place in the four food groups and provides a good substitute for red meat in the meat group.

If you eat seafood twice a week, you can cut down on calories and add variety to your eating habits. Variety is the essence of good nutrition, and seafood, in particular, provides a sound complement of protein, minerals, and fats to give you the balance you need.

(The following verse was translated from the French of Elie Marcuse, Paris, 1938.)

THE ENVIOUS CRAB

The crab surveyed the ocean floor.
Above him, swimming by the score,
Were fish, who moved with utmost grace.
The envious crab, with downcast face,
Cried to himself this plaintive word:
Why am I not, like them, a bird?

»« INDEX